CHANGES AND CHALLENGES
BECOMING THE BEST YOU CAN BE

Articles and stories contributed by:

Gary R. Collins

Bill Cosby

Rick Little

Peggy Mann

Charlie Shedd

W. Clement Stone

Barbara Varenhorst

THIRD EDITION

SKILLS FOR ADOLESCENCE
Lions-Quest

**A Joint Program of
Lions Clubs International
and Quest International**

Sponsored in part by a generous contribution
from the W.K. Kellogg Foundation

PROGRAM DEVELOPMENT STAFF FOR QUEST INTERNATIONAL

Founder and Chairman: Rick Little

President and CEO: David A. Spencer

Vice President of Training: Joyce E. Phelps

Vice President for Program Development: Susan Carroll Keister

Senior Writers: Carol Apacki and Linda Barr

Writers: Anita Hamm and Hank Resnik

Director of Creative Services: Wendy Hollinger Peters

Art Director: Rhonda R. Sellers

Senior Editor: Dale Anne Hambrecht

Editor: Chrisa Hotchkiss

Production Editor: Stanley J. Sobiech

Production Manager: Lynne K. Taylor

Production Assistants: Jodi Cullins and Tracy Saunders

Photographers: Todd Yarrington and Kent Miles

Illustrator: Estella Hickman

Text Illustrator: Ron Lieser

Medical Illustrator: Gina Urwin

A Book About You

Welcome to a new program! You're about to become one of many thousands of students from around the world to be involved in a very special program. This program focuses on the concerns, hopes, dreams, and goals of people your age. It's called the Lions-Quest *Skills for Adolescence* program, and it's about you!

In the *Skills for Adolescence* program you will discuss the changes you're experiencing during this important time in your life. You'll learn how to strengthen your self-confidence, manage your emotions, and communicate better with friends and family members. There's plenty of practice in decision making and problem solving, too. You'll learn ways being healthy and drug-free will help you become the person you were meant to be—and ways to stay drug-free and help others stay drug-free. Finally, you'll practice setting goals and thinking about ways to make the most of yourself.

This book is divided into nine sections, one for each unit of *Skills for Adolescence,* plus one for Service Learning. It's filled with activities, assignments, articles, and stories that will help you learn more about the topics discussed in class.

So enjoy the program! We hope you, like thousands of other young people, find *Skills for Adolescence,* plus one for service learning a rewarding experience. You have our warmest wishes for your success this year and in years to come.

Your Friends at Lions Clubs International
and Quest International

A Note About Lions Clubs International and Quest International

Lions Clubs International is the largest service organization in the world, with more than 1.6 million members in nearly 170 countries. Lions have provided major funding for the Lions-Quest *Skills for Adolescence* program for the middle grades and the Lions-Quest *Skills for Growing* program for students in grades K–5. These two programs are major components of the Lions' long-term commitment to drug education and awareness.

Quest International is a nonprofit organization that was founded in 1975 and specializes in programs for positive youth development. In addition to *Skills for Adolescence* and *Skills for Growing,* Quest is creating a new course in life skills for high-school-aged young people.

Quest International is a founding member of the National Coalition for the Prevention of Drug and Alcohol Abuse and is funded by dozens of foundations, corporations, and contributions from those who support its work with young people. For more information contact Quest International, 537 Jones Road, P.O. Box 566, Granville, Ohio 43023-0566. Contact Lions-Quest Canada at 515 Dotzert Court, Unit #7, Waterloo, Ontario N2L 6A7.

TABLE OF CONTENTS

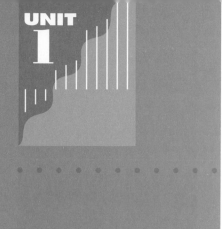

UNIT 1
ENTERING THE TEEN YEARS:
THE CHALLENGE AHEAD

We asked a group of 13-year-olds how they felt about entering adolescence. Here are some of their answers:

There are so many changes. You go from being a little kid to being an adult. You start having dances and girlfriends, things you dreamed of when you were eight years old. You have more responsibilities. Your teachers teach you new things that you aren't really ready to learn. You leave elementary school, where you had one teacher and easy homework, and find yourself with six teachers and much harder homework. There are just too many changes at one time.

I feel like I'm on an emotional roller coaster. Sometimes I just want to go outside and do the things I did when I was little. And other times I just want to crawl into a hole and cry until I can't cry any more. One minute I'm acting really normal, and the next I'm yelling and taking out my anger on everyone around me.

It really bothers me when adults treat you like a little kid but expect you to act like an adult. You ask them if you can do something and they say, "You are too young." Then if you do something wrong, they say, "Why are you so irresponsible?" or "You're old enough to know better than that." It can really get confusing."

Do any of these thoughts and feelings sound familiar to you? If they do, you're not alone. All people your age are experiencing what's called "early adolescence."

It's a special time in your life. Many things are happening to your body, your feelings, and your relationships with your friends and family. Some days you may feel as if you're going through more changes more quickly than you've ever experienced before. Well, you are!

You're in a wonderful period when you're bridging the gap between childhood and adulthood. Much of the time you may feel like a child and an adult at the same time. This is normal. This unit is designed to help you understand, accept, and enjoy this period in your life to the fullest. You'll begin by getting to know your classmates better and helping to set ground rules so everyone will treat one another with respect. (No put-downs allowed!) Discussions about the normal changes of adolescence will help clear up some points you may have wondered about. You'll also begin to explore how peer pressure affects your life and identify skills that will help you make the most of early adolescence.

The article titled "Look What's Happening—A New Me!" was written by Bill Cosby, a father, educator, and well-known comedian. He describes the many changes adolescents experience. The main point of the article is that you're not alone, and no matter how "different" you feel, what you're experiencing is normal.

The short story for this unit is called "Clothes Encounters." It tells about a 12-year-old girl who returns from summer vacation to find she's suddenly taller than most of her friends. The story shows us that sometimes the changes of adolescence can be painful, but love and understanding can make those changes easier.

GETTING STARTED

Read the quotations again. Do you agree with any of them? In the space below, explain what *you* would say if someone asked how you feel about entering early adolescence.

_____

_____

_____

_____

_____

_____

_____

_____

UNIT 1
UNIT PROJECTS

Complete at least one unit project by working on your own, with a partner, or with the class.

1. Design a logo or insignia for your *Skills for Adolescence* class that could be used on T-shirts, notebooks, and so on.

2. Collect articles, cartoons, and pictures related to the unit—for example, the challenges and changes of adolescence. Organize them in a notebook and share them with the class. Write a sentence explaining how each picture illustrates a concept from the unit.

3. Write a short story about one of the unit themes. Share it with your family and/or class members. Examples:
   • A young adolescent deals with the changes in his or her life.
   • A group of teenagers learns how to stop putting each other down.
   • A teenager worries about the first day in a new school, but meets new friends.

4. Modify a class activity and use it at home with your family. Talk with your teacher about which activity you will use. Write a report explaining:
   • What you did
   • How it worked
   • How it was helpful to you and other family members
   • How you would improve the activity if you did it again

   In your report, be sure to respect the privacy of your family members. Ask them to read your report and okay it before you bring it to school.

5. Ask three students and three adults this question: "What are three things you like about being your present age?" Write down their responses and present them to your class, without naming the people you interviewed. Discuss any similarities and differences you found.

PEOPLE SEARCH

NAME: _____ DATE: _____

Find a different person in the class to fit each description and ask him or her to initial that box.

Find someone who has lived in another state or province. Which one?	Find someone who gets up by 8:00 on Saturday mornings.	Find someone who owns an unusual pet. What is it?
Find someone who has a birthday in the same month as yours. Which month is it?	Find someone who plays a musical instrument. Which instrument?	Find someone who collects something. What is collected?
Find someone who has read a good book lately. What is the title?	Find someone who lives near you. What is that person's address?	Find someone whose favorite sport is baseball.
Find someone who has won a contest. What kind of contest?	Find someone who plays a sport after school. What is the sport?	Find someone who is as tall as you are. How tall are you both?
Find someone who	Find someone who	Find someone who

Different strokes for different folks.

7

CLASSROOM GROUND RULES

NAME: _____ DATE: _____

Write the final list of rules your class and your teacher chose.

1. _____
   _____
   _____
   _____

2. _____
   _____
   _____
   _____
   _____

3. _____
   _____
   _____
   _____
   _____

4. _____
   _____
   _____
   _____
   _____

5. _____
   _____
   _____
   _____

6. _____
   _____
   _____
   _____

When you are good to others, you are best to yourself. —Benjamin Franklin

WHAT WOULD CHANGE?

NAME: _____ DATE: _____

• •

If everyone followed the ground rules in all your classes, what are some things that would change? List at least four ways your classes would be different.

1. _____
   _____
   _____
   _____
   _____

2. _____
   _____
   _____
   _____
   _____

3. _____
   _____
   _____
   _____
   _____

4. _____
   _____
   _____
   _____
   _____

Be cool, follow the rules.

DIONARAPS

NAME: _____ DATE: _____

SOME DIONARAPS TO TRY

| Clip out a newspaper cartoon that you think will make someone laugh and give or send it to that person. |

| Send a humorous card to someone on a day other than a holiday or the person's birthday. |

| Say hello and smile at ten new people at school in one day. |

| Throw a surprise "unbirthday" party for a friend or family member. |

| During a conversation say, "To be honest with you..." —then say something positive. |

A fun way to build people up is to help them become "Dionaraps." *Dionarap* is *paranoid* spelled backwards. Being a Dionarap is the opposite of being paranoid. When people are paranoid, they think that everyone else is out to get them. Dionaraps are people who think the world is out to do them good.

You can help others become Dionaraps by making some unexpected, friendly gesture, or helping them out in a small, unexpected way. To the left are some ideas you can use to help family members, friends, and even people you don't know very well become Dionaraps.

Be sure that any humor you use will make another person feel good. It shouldn't be humor that might be taken as a put-down.

On the lines below, write down three more ways you can help people become Dionaraps. Try out your ideas tonight.

1. _____

   _____

2. _____

   _____

3. _____

   _____

At home tonight, explain to your family what a Dionarap is. Share with them some ideas on how to help others become Dionaraps. Ask a parent or another adult to think of ways they can help friends, coworkers, and even total strangers become Dionaraps everyday. For example, they could hold a door for someone or let someone go ahead of them in a checkout line. Write three of their ideas.

_____

_____

_____

_____

Ask how they feel after doing one of the things they described above.

_____

Did you feel the same way after trying some of your ideas?

_____

One good turn deserves another.

Boostergram

NAME: _____ DATE: _____

BOOSTERGRAM:

Date: _____

To: _____

Message:_____

_____

_____

_____

_____

_____

_____

From: _____

BOOSTERGRAM:

Date: _____

To: _____

Message:_____

_____

_____

_____

_____

_____

_____

From: _____

SPECIAL DELIVERY

To:_____
_____
_____
_____
_____
_____
_____
_____

SPECIAL DELIVERY

To:_____
_____
_____
_____
_____
_____
_____
_____

INTERVIEW FORM

NAME: _____ DATE: _____

· ·

Interview your partner to gather this information.

Partner's full name: _____

Nickname: _____

Birthdate: _____

Birthplace: _____

Favorite book: _____

Favorite magazine: _____

Favorite television show: _____

Favorite actor/actress: _____

Favorite singer: _____

Favorite song: _____

Favorite sport: _____

Favorite subject in school: _____

Favorite food: _____

Favorite hobbies/pastimes: _____

Favorite place: _____

Favorite saying: _____

Ambition in life: _____

Favorite family activity: _____

_____

_____

_____

_____

_____

There are no strangers here—only friends we haven't met.

A TIME OF CHANGES

Complete the puzzle.

WORD BOX

SPURT
HORMONES
INTELLECTUAL
INFANT
BALANCED
ABSTRACT
NUTRITION
AWKWARD
TEMPORARY
NEGATIVE
ADOLESCENCE
CONCRETE
ADULTS
EMOTIONS
PHYSICAL
GLANDS
BONES

ACROSS

3. The period between childhood and adulthood is called _____.
5. Candy, soft drinks, and snacks do not make a _____ diet.
7. Good _____ helps adolescents reach their full height and weight.
10. Adolescents' _____ can change rapidly.
12. A period of rapid development is called a growth _____.
13. Young children use _____ thinking, relying on what they can see, hear, or touch.
14. Because of their rapid growth, adolescents may feel _____.
15. Adolescents experience many _____ changes in their bodies.

DOWN

1. Adolescents also experience rapid _____ development, changing the way they think.
2. One physical change is the development of sweat _____.
3. Adolescents learn to use _____ thinking to do difficult math problems.
4. Chemicals that control physical growth are called _____.
5. During adolescence, _____ often grow faster than muscles.
6. Resisting _____ influences is a great challenge facing adolescents.
8. An adolescent's body changes as quickly as when he or she was an _____.
9. Adolescents begin to look like they will when they're _____.
11. Some changes, such as acne, are only _____.

PEER PRESSURE SURVEY

• •

Read each statement carefully. Put an X in the box that shows how often this situation happens.

	Never	Once a Month	2 or More Times a Month
1. My peers pressure me to smoke cigarettes.	☐	☐	☐
2. My peers pressure me to drink alcohol.	☐	☐	☐
3. My peers use drugs and expect me to.	☐	☐	☐
4. My peers ask me to cheat at school.	☐	☐	☐
5. My peers follow school rules and expect me to follow them.	☐	☐	☐
6. My peers ask me to shoplift.	☐	☐	☐
7. My peers ask me to call people names or be cruel to others.	☐	☐	☐
8. My peers encourage me to be thoughtful of others.	☐	☐	☐
9. My peers ask me to do things my family disapproves of.	☐	☐	☐
10. My peers follow their families' rules and expect me to follow my family's rules.	☐	☐	☐
11. My peers stand up to negative peer pressure.	☐	☐	☐
12. My peers ask me to join them in drug-free activities.	☐	☐	☐
13. My peers _____	☐	☐	☐
14. My peers _____	☐	☐	☐
15. My peers _____	☐	☐	☐

15

WHAT'S AHEAD?

NAME: _____ DATE: _____

Identify one goal in each category below and describe specific ways you plan to reach it.

PHYSICAL CHANGES

Goal: _____

Plan: _____

_____

_____

_____

SOCIAL CHANGES

Goal: _____

Plan: _____

_____

_____

_____

INTELLECTUAL OR ACADEMIC CHANGES

Goal: _____

Plan: _____

_____

_____

_____

EMOTIONAL CHANGES

Goal: _____

Plan: _____

_____

_____

_____

Strive to make something of yourselves; then strive to make the most of yourselves. —Alexander Crumwell

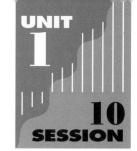

LOOK WHAT'S HAPPENING— A NEW ME!

BY BILL COSBY

Hi, boys and girls! I'm Bill Cosby.

Wait a minute. Whoa! "Boys and girls"? That's baby stuff. You guys aren't babies. Let me start all over again.

Hi, men and women. I'm Bill . . . .

Now, "men and women" is closer. But it's not right either. Let me try another one. Just one more. I promise. Here goes.

Hi, people between the ages of 10 and 14 who are probably in grade six, seven, or eight! I'm Bill . . . .

Whew! I'm having trouble just getting started. And I thought getting started would be the easy part.

Well, let's not fuss over what we call you. If you're between the ages of 10 and 14, you're at a time of life known as early adolescence. Some people in grade six are still very young, more like children than adults. Others are starting to grow up. They're not adults, but they're not exactly children any more either. Some kids in grades seven and eight look and act like young men and women.

Whatever you call yourself (I usually just call myself "Bill"), early adolescence is a time when all kinds of exciting changes are happening in your life. That's part of what this book is about: changes.

THE CHANGES BEGIN

One of the biggest changes in early adolescence is what's called a growth spurt. At this point in your life, your body is either growing or about to grow faster than at any time except when you were a baby. Another word for this is *puberty*. It's the time when young people first become able to reproduce. They start to be like adults in many other ways, too.

It all happens because of chemicals called *hormones,* which send messages to the different parts of your body telling them how to grow. All kinds of changes are going on in your body during adolescence. They include changes in your brain, skin, bones, and muscles, for example. The shape of your body changes. Boys become stronger, girls more curvy.

But people in early adolescence don't all change the same way at the same time. Some shoot up and look as if they're going to turn into giants. When this happens, their aunts and uncles and grandparents always say one of three things:

1. "My, how you've grown! I remember when I picked you up and bounced you on my knee."
2. "I can't get over how you've grown! I remember when I picked you up and bounced you on my knee."

"My, how you've grown! I remember when I picked you up and bounced you on my knee."

3. "You certainly have shot up! You're going to be bigger than your (mother/father/brother/sister), and I remember when I used to pick (him/her) up and bounce (him/her) on my knee."

While some people's uncles and aunts and grandparents are saying these things, other people's uncles and aunts and grandparents are saying "Finish your spinach so you'll grow a little. Your cousin Stephanie is a whole head taller than you, and she's only nine!"

A healthy, balanced diet *is* very important during adolescence, but eating spinach won't make you grow two inches overnight. You'll just have to be patient.

You might be interested to know that adolescents as a group are getting bigger than they used to. The typical adolescent of today is much bigger than the typical adolescent of 100 years ago.

Why is this happening? So far no scientist has discovered that it's the result of listening to loud music and eating french fries. But don't give up hope. Actually, it's more likely to be the result of eating foods that are good for you (despite all those french fries). Also, today we have better health care than they had 100 years ago.

Another interesting thing about the changes of adolescence is that they aren't always logical. Your feet and head may reach their adult size long before the rest of you, for example. It may take your torso a while to catch up with your legs. As a result, adolescence—especially early adolescence—can be a gangly period when you tend to bump into things.

> *Probably every adolescent wants to be normal, although some worry about it more than others. The problem is that "normal" means many things among adolescents! At no other time of life are people the same age so different from each other.*

Probably every adolescent wants to be normal, although some worry about it more than others. The problem is that "normal" means many things among adolescents! At no other time of life are people the same age so different from each other. An adolescent whose growth spurt begins very early is normal. So is the one whose growth spurt begins very late. The tall ones are normal; so are the short ones. Some adolescents get zits; some don't. Adolescents come in all sizes and shapes. That's part of what makes it one of the most interesting, surprising, and sometimes frustrating times of life.

As if these changes weren't puzzling enough, boys and girls change at very different rates. Most girls begin to mature about two years before boys. This can be difficult for everyone, especially the girls' parents, when the girls would rather be driving around with 16-year-olds than hanging out with kids their own age.

MORE CHANGES IN YOU

Adolescence can be the most horrible time of your life. Your favorite clothes shrink so quickly, your hair never does what you want it to, and you never know what to say until ten minutes after you should have said it.

On the other hand, adolescence can be the most exciting time of your whole life. You start to really think about who you are and who you want to be. This is normal. Try this simple exercise:

Stand in front of a full-length mirror. Say to the mirror: "Who am I? Who have I been in the past? Who will I become? What do I like or dislike about myself?"

If your mirror doesn't give you some very good answers within five minutes, it may be defective.

Adolescence may be the time when you have your first really best friend. You're so important to each other that you have to spend at least an hour on the phone right after school telling each other all the things you forgot to say on the way home.

When you're an adolescent it may seem as if the sun is setting just for you. Because of that, sunsets are more beautiful than they've ever been before.

Adolescence is a time of the most incredible range of feelings. One moment you're up. The next moment you're down. You may even feel sometimes that someone or something else is in control of your feelings—not you. This gets back to all the physical changes in your body and those things called hormones. They cause big emotional changes, too. All of these changes are normal.

CHANGES IN SCHOOL

So, you're in a new school. Suddenly you have four or five different teachers instead of one—and every one of them assigns at least two hours of homework every night. You don't need to work out to get into shape. All you have to do is carry your books around with you!

School is no longer child's play. It's hard work. But most kids say to themselves, "Okay, schoolwork isn't always going to be fun. But if I want to make something of myself, I need an education."

You don't have to be really smart to know this, and you don't have to be really smart to do well in school. You *do* have to work, though. Even the smartest kids have to work, although it may look easy for them.

Are you afraid of school? This may sound strange, but many people do develop such a fear. They begin to think they can't do well in school, and the more they think this is so, the worse they do. Are you afraid to try? If you don't try, you won't risk failing, of course. But is that really the easy way out?

Part of the reason school may seem harder is that teachers and other adults are demanding more from you. They expect you to think more like an adult than a child. But you can do it!

You see, adolescents start to think differently from younger kids. They can figure out more difficult math problems. When they really put some effort into it, they can tell better jokes. They can remember much more than young children. Also, their vocabularies become much bigger. Even so, many adolescents seem to get by with just a few words. These include "Like, wow," "Cool," "Gross," "Yuck," "Awesome," "Hey, dude," and "How much?"

The new levels of thinking you develop in adolescence may amaze you. All of a sudden it may seem that you never really noticed the world before. Things may begin to make sense to you that you never understood.

All the great inventions of the modern world are the result of the kind of creative thinking you can do now for the first time in your life.

Let's look at an example of how your thinking changes when your mind matures. Imagine that you poured some water into a short, fat glass and then poured the same amount of water into a tall, skinny glass. The level of water would be higher in the second glass. A three-year-old might tell you the second glass contains more water because it's higher. The more mature thinker recognizes that the amount of water is the same. The more mature thinker is capable of what we call *abstract thinking.*

The three-year-old can only tell you what he or she actually sees. In adolescence, you're able to think things out in a much more adult way. You can make connections between things (people, ideas, objects) just by thinking about them. This is something a young child can't do.

All the great inventions of the modern world are the result of the kind of creative thinking you can do now for the first time in your life.

THE CHALLENGES OF ADOLESCENCE

Adolescence is full of changes, and it's full of challenges. It seems that every time you walk around a corner (either in school or in your own life), there's a new decision to make or a new problem to solve. Here are some of the tasks you'll have to do to pass through adolescence successfully:

• Develop more grown-up relationships with people of both sexes.

• Begin to become an adult.

• Accept your body and learn how to respect and take care of it.

• Begin to prepare for the work you will do after school.

Don't panic—you don't have to accomplish all these things by next week. But most young people reach these goals by the time they're in their late teens.

One of the biggest challenges kids your age face is pressure to use alcohol, tobacco, and other drugs. That pressure is too much for a few young people. They haven't learned to say "No."

Some kids start using drugs (usually cigarettes, beer, or wine coolers at first) because they think it makes them look more grown-up or cool. Others do it because they think everyone else is doing it. They don't want to feel left out—even though they don't like the taste or smell or how drugs make them feel.

But the fact is, most kids *don't* do drugs. Later in this book you'll learn lots of reasons why. Using them can be a quick way to ruin your life. You may know or hear of people whose lives are being ruined by drugs. Once these people probably thought smoking, drinking, and using other drugs was grown-up and cool. Sad, isn't it?

RELATIONSHIPS WITH ADULTS

A lot of people talk about a generation gap between youth and adults. They say it gets widest when young people are going through adolescence. There's some truth to this. It's normal for adolescents to want to make their own decisions and be as independent as possible. Parents who have been loving and helpful all your life can suddenly seem *too* helpful. But remember, it's hard for them, too. After all these years of taking care of you and being responsible for you, it's not easy to let go.

As an adolescent, it's important for you to find adults you respect and admire. Strange as it may seem, someday you'll be an adult too. Chances are that unless you're extremely unusual, you'll grow up to be a lot like the adults you know—your parents or other people you like and admire.

Growing up means a lot more than staying up as late as you want. It means deciding what kind of adult you want to be and taking some responsibility for your life.

It means working to become the happy, healthy person you want to be.

If that sounds good to you, keep reading and keep thinking. This book can help you chart your course!

• •

FACTUAL QUESTIONS:

1. Why doesn't Bill Cosby think it's a good idea to call you "boys and girls"?

_____

2. How many different changes of early adolescence does the article describe?

_____

3. What are hormones?

_____

4. How is the typical adolescent of today different from the typical adolescent of 100 years ago?

_____

5. According to the article, what are some of the challenges of adolescence? The joys?

_____

_____

6. What changes in school and schoolwork are mentioned?

_____

7. What does Bill Cosby think about teenagers using alcohol and other drugs? Find sentences in the book to support your answer.

_____

_____

INTERPRETIVE QUESTIONS:

8. What are some benefits of identifying adults in your life you respect and admire? What can you learn from them?

_____

_____

9. If you were to summarize Bill Cosby's main message in a few sentences, what would you say?

_____

_____

Grant me the courage to change those things I can;
Grant me the patience to accept those things I can't change;
Grant me the wisdom to know the difference.

THOUGHTS ABOUT YOUTH

Ask a parent or another adult to read the following quotations and proverbs with you. Then answer the questions at the bottom of the page.

Be content with such things as you have. —The Bible

A young branch takes on all the bends that one gives it. —Chinese proverb

How beautiful is youth! How bright its gleams
With its illusion, aspiration, dreams!
—Henry Wadsworth Longfellow, American poet

For young people today things move so fast there is no problem of adjustment. Before you can adjust to A, B has appeared leading C by the hand, and with D in the distance. —Louis Kronenberger, writer

One's work may be finished some day, but one's education never. —Alexandre Dumas, French writer

A sure way for one to lift himself up is by helping to lift someone else. —Booker T. Washington, American educator

A youth is to be regarded with respect. How do you know that his future will not be equal to our present? —Confucius, Chinese philosopher

He who would learn to fly one day must first learn to stand and walk and run and climb and dance; one cannot fly into flying. —F. W. Nietzsche, German philosopher

If you refuse to be made straight when you are green, you will not be made straight when you are dry. —African proverb

Remember that as a teenager you are in the last stage of your life when you will be happy to hear that the phone is for you. —Fran Lebowitz, American journalist

By wise people, an appropriate observation is accepted even from a child. On the invisibility of the sun, is not the light of a lamp availed of? —Sanskrit proverb

1. Which quotation do you like best? What message does it express?

_____

_____

_____

2. Which quotation does the adult like best? What message does it express?

_____

_____

_____

3. Ask the adult to think of another proverb or saying about being young or growing up that is especially helpful or appropriate. If you or the adult speak another language, you might want to write a saying in that language.

_____

_____

_____

SKILLS TO BUILD ON

NAME: _____ DATE: _____

Have your partner fill in this worksheet as you explain your answers.

Two "skills for adolescence" I need to improve are:

1. _____
   _____
   _____

2. _____
   _____
   _____

Two ways I can improve each of these skills are:

SKILL 1:

1. _____
   _____
   _____

2. _____
   _____
   _____

SKILL 2:

1. _____
   _____
   _____

2. _____
   _____
   _____

Two good things that may happen when I improve these skills are:

1. _____
   _____
   _____

2. _____
   _____
   _____

To achieve all that is possible, we must attempt the impossible; to be as much as we can be, we must dream of being more.

CLOTHES ENCOUNTERS

Lisa felt a tap on her shoulder and turned around. It was Donnie Phillips, one of the coolest guys in the class, holding out a slip of paper.

"Pass it to Judy," he said. But the smirk on his face said, "Boy, what happened to you over the summer? You used to be okay, but now you're tall and ugly."

Lisa reached out and grabbed the slip of paper.

Suddenly a voice snapped, "Lisa! Donnie! What's going on there?"

Lisa twisted her arm in a big circle and plunked her hand down on the social studies quiz in front of her. Then she continued writing as if she'd just been getting a kink out of her arm. "Nothing, Mrs. Sikorsky," she said in a weary-sounding voice. "Tired arm."

Mrs. Sikorsky didn't look convinced. "You had better get back to work. You have only ten minutes left."

Lisa finished her quiz early, but she didn't dare look at the note. Only when the bell rang and she filed out of class with the other kids did she get up the nerve to open it. The note said:

> Judy—
> She's wearing purple eye shadow. And a
> purple skirt. And purple shoes. Gross!
> —Lynn

From the hallway, Lisa turned around to look back at Mrs. Sikorsky. It was true. Purple, purple, purple. She wasn't sure it was all that gross, though. She liked Mrs. Sikorsky, who was fairly young for a teacher and kind of pretty. Then Lisa noticed that even Mrs. Sikorsky was shorter than she was now—like most people in the world!

Lisa sighed and looked at the note in her hand. A little voice in the back of her mind whispered, "Last year Lynn passed notes to you. This year she passes them to Judy. But you and Lynn are supposed to be best friends. So much for best friends!"

"Oh, just shut up!" Lisa muttered. All at once she could feel her face getting as hot as if she were sunburned. She had actually said that aloud! She couldn't believe it—she was talking to herself!

Just at that moment, two girls had passed her in the hall going the opposite way. They were only a few steps behind her when she heard their giggles. Her face felt even hotter.

"You're so big," said the obnoxious little voice inside her head. "You could probably pick up both of them and knock their silly heads together. Of course, that would make you look even more stupid than you look already."

The rest of the day dragged by. Lisa headed for the front door of the school as soon as the last bell rang.

"Lisa! Over here!" her mom called.

Lisa hurried across the front lawn of the school toward her mother's car, opened the door, and flung herself inside. Then she realized that Jimmy, her little brother (half-brother, actually), had moved the seat forward again and she was all scrunched up. She groped for the handle and slid the seat back as far as it would go.

"How was school?" Lisa's mother asked as they drove off.

"Fine."

"Everything okay? Ready to do some shopping?"

"Uh huh."

"It's wonderful to hear so much news about school," her mother said, half-joking. Lisa pretended she hadn't heard this, and for a while they drove to the mall in silence.

"Can I get some of those jeans with buttons instead of a zipper?" Lisa finally asked. "They're so neat. But there's only one kind that's really good. Lynn's mom says the other brand falls apart."

"Sure, if they're not too expensive," her mother answered. "By the way, how *is* Lynn? I haven't seen her for a while. Did she have a good summer?"

"She's okay. She went to the camp that Judy and Phyllis went to. The one where you get to ride horses every day. And she went to her grandmother's house. But that was boring."

"Uh huh."

Lisa wondered if her mother could tell she'd picked up this information by overhearing Lynn and Judy in the hall. She wondered if her mother knew Lynn wasn't her best friend any more, that something terrible had happened over the summer. Mainly, she'd turned into this giant that everybody laughed at and nobody liked.

Lisa was relieved to see that the mall was almost empty. Lots of kids came to the mall after school, but they weren't here yet.

"How about the department store?" her mother asked. "They'd probably have those jeans."

"No, the store next to the place with all the running and tennis clothes has them. I heard . . . some of the kids told me about it."

The real question, she thought, was whether they would have the jeans she wanted in her size. Her great big colossal gigantic huge size, whatever it was.

She'd had a dream a few days ago. In the dream she and her mom went into a department store, and the clerk took out a huge ruler to measure her with. Then the clerk practically yelled, "This girl is so tall that we don't have anything to fit her. She'll have to go to the giants' department."

In the dream they'd gone home without buying any clothes. Then her mother had made some horrible tacky pants and tops on her sewing machine, out of old rags. And when she wore the rags to school and walked down the hallway, all of her classmates lined up on either side, laughing as she passed by.

But, to her surprise, shopping turned out a lot better than her dream. Not only did the store have the jeans she wanted in a size that fit, but her mother helped her pick out three brightly colored tops that were on sale. For the first time that day she felt almost happy.

Then the clerk spoiled it. As he was putting the clothes in a bag, he smiled at Lisa's mother and said, "They sure are growing them bigger these days, aren't they?"

"Her father's tall," said Lisa's petite mother. "Very tall."

The afternoon was ruined. The year was ruined. Lisa felt like crying, but she pretended everything was normal as they headed back to the car.

"I have to stop at the grocery store," her mother said. "Do you want to come along?"

Lisa shook her head. "I have to do some homework."

"Okay. I'll just take you home first."

After her mother dropped her off, Lisa was relieved to find that she had the house to herself, at least for the time being. Her older brother Allen must have had a meeting or something after school. And she knew her younger brother Jimmy was at soccer practice.

She ran up to her room and threw herself on the bed. After lying there for several minutes and trying to make her mind a blank, she reached for the bag of clothes and dumped it on her bed. There they were. Giant's clothes. Clothes for the towering geek.

She shoved the clothes onto the floor. "I hate you! I hate you!"

This time her tears really flowed. After a while her pillow was wet, and she felt something fluffy brushing against her.

"Hi, Amanda," Lisa said to the orange cat. "You're so lucky you're small. Me, I'm like Alice in Wonderland when she grows so tall that she fills up a whole room." The cat rubbed against her, purring like an outboard motor. Lisa smiled through her tears. "I'm suffering and you demand to be petted. You're incredibly, unbelievably selfish. But I love you anyway."

Lisa was startled by a soft knock at her door. Then the door opened, and her half-brother Allen stuck his head in.

"This girl is so tall that we don't have anything to fit her. She'll have to go to the giants' department."

"I couldn't help overhearing." His smile revealed a mouthful of straight white teeth, now that his braces were off. "You love me even though I'm unbelievably selfish. Thank you, thank you, thank you!"

Lisa picked up the pillow and hurled it at him. "Ooh, you weren't supposed to be listening!" He ducked to avoid the pillow. Then, picking it up, he came into the room and bowed.

"Excuse me, ma'am, but I believe you dropped your pillow."

Lisa grabbed the pillow and hit him over the head with it several times.

"Murder! The great pillow massacre!" Allen shouted. Then, with a sudden lunge, he grabbed the pillow from her and began to pound her with it.

"I give up! I give up!" Lisa shouted through her laughter.

Breathing hard, she grinned at him. He looked back at her through his tousled brown hair. With his turned-up smile, dimpled cheeks, and slightly oversized ears, he looked like a jaunty elf. He was 17 and had a great sense of humor. All in all, he was pretty fun to have around. Lisa had concluded earlier that he was the main benefit of her mother's second marriage.

Allen's smile disappeared as he examined the pillow he was still holding. "Someone," he said in an exaggeratedly serious voice, "has been crying on your pillow." He picked up one of the blouses from the floor. "And someone has been throwing clothes around." He sniffed the air like a comic detective. "I sink somesing iss wrong here." He smiled his great big toothy grin and stood there waiting for her to speak.

Lisa concentrated on picking invisible specks of lint from her jeans. There were lots of them.

"If you don't want to talk about it, I bet I can guess," Allen finally said.

"I bet you can't. Nobody understands what I'm going through, not even you."

"Well, officially I, too, am still a teenager. Even though I look and act like a dashing young man."

"You're a boy!"

"Sometimes. But I am especially sensitive. That means girls think I'm cute and like to talk to me. Being short and cute and sensitive has its advantages."

Lisa still didn't look at him, but she mumbled, "Well, being tall and . . . taller than anybody else in the class when you happen to be a girl has no advantages that I can see. Starting with your short friends not liking you anymore."

For a while there was more silence. She looked up, and Allen's bright blue eyes held hers in a lock.

"Remember last year," he asked, "when I had that physical before I went to be a counselor at that camp?"

• •

She nodded.

"That's when I finally asked Dr. Grant a question I'd been worried about for years," Allen went on. "'Doc,' I said, 'I'm one of the shortest guys in my class, and I feel lousy about it. Am I going to grow any more?'"

Lisa almost stopped breathing as she waited for him to continue.

Allen smiled at the memory. "It was hard to ask him that, believe me. I was so nervous I thought maybe I was going to throw up or something. But I figured he'd know."

"What did he say?"

"He took me over to this chart on the wall that showed growth patterns. Then he told me I was in about the tenth percentile. That means 90 percent of the guys my age would be taller than me. And he told me I'd passed my growth spurt, so I probably wouldn't grow a lot taller. He said he wouldn't recommend a career in basketball!"

Lisa was horrified. "What a terrible thing to say!"

"Not at all," Allen said. "He was being honest. He didn't want me kidding myself. Of course, I was kind of upset at first. I mean, I want to be normal. I want to be like the other guys my age, so I was pretty shook up.

"Then he put both hands on my shoulders and stood there looking me in the eye. 'The world is made up of tall people, short people, white people, black people—all kinds of people,' he said. 'You are what you are. You can spend the rest of your life wanting to be something else. Or you can accept who you are and be a happy person who will bring love and happiness to others. You can choose for yourself.'"

For a while Lisa couldn't say anything. Then all she said was "Wow!"

"Yeah," said Allen. "Wow. I'll never forget it. Never." He jumped up and stood there smiling. "That's why you see me as I am. On the small side, but otherwise perfect." He beckoned to her. "Stand up."

"No!"

"Stand up!" he ordered. She stood.

"Look at you, you little twerp," he said. "You aren't as tall as I am. You're a shrimp."

Lisa didn't know whether to laugh or cry. "I'm . . . I'm gigantic. The other girls think I'm a freak."

"They're probably jealous because they're even shrimpier than you are," Allen said with a mischievous chuckle. "They know that the basketball types—people who are even taller than I am—will prefer you to them."

"Oh, sure!"

"It's true." He smiled as he headed for the door. "We older people know these things!"

"'Doc,' I said, 'I'm one of the shortest guys in my class, and I feel lousy about it. Am I going to grow any more?'"

29

After Allen closed the bedroom door behind him, Lisa picked the pink blouse up off the floor and changed into it.

Slowly she turned to look at herself in the mirror.

"This really doesn't look that bad," she admitted. "Maybe there's hope for me after all. I bet I could do something new with my hair, too."

She grinned at her reflection as she reached for her brush.

FACTUAL QUESTIONS:

1. What are some things Lisa feels self-conscious about? Why are these things so important to her?

_____

_____

2. What do Lisa and Allen talk about?

_____

3. What did Allen's doctor tell him about accepting his height? What was Allen's reaction?

_____

_____

4. What effect does this conversation have on Lisa?

_____

_____

• •

INTERPRETIVE QUESTIONS:

5. What emotions has Lisa experienced during this one day? Why do you think such mood swings are typical of early adolescence?

_____

_____

_____

6. What solutions to the changes and challenges of adolescence are offered in the story?

_____

_____

_____

TIPS: *So you're going through a lot of changes, right? Well, you can make changes into challenges and challenges into successes. Here are some points to keep in mind during this time of changes in your life:*

- *Believe in yourself.*

- *Try to do the best you can—always.*

- *Don't forget that developing your potential in life means making healthy decisions right now.*

- *Take care of your health and hygiene—they're an important part of who you are.*

- *Remember that your image is more than the way you look—it has a lot to do with the way you think.*

- *Remember that there are caring adults to help you during these years!*

- *Give yourself the chance to become the best you can be. Stay drug-free!*

LOOKING BACK

NAME: _____ DATE: _____

Use what you've learned during this unit to write a letter to someone in grade five. Explain at least four changes he or she can expect during early adolescence. Then name at least one "skill for adolescence" that will help this younger person handle each change successfully. Before starting your letter, list the changes and skills you've chosen.

1. Change: _____

_____

   Skill: _____

_____

2. Change: _____

_____

   Skill: _____

_____

3. Change: _____

_____

   Skill: _____

_____

4. Change: _____

_____

   Skill: _____

_____

YOUR LETTER:

UNIT 2
BUILDING SELF-CONFIDENCE AND COMMUNICATION SKILLS

Many people think self-confidence is the key to a happy, successful life. But where does self-confidence come from? How can you hang on to it for more than five minutes? Here's what some students have to say about it:

Self-confidence means proving to myself that I can do something well. It's even better if someone else tells you that you're good at something, too.

When people listen to me and pay attention to my ideas, I know they like me. When people don't listen, I sometimes feel rejected. Listening shows they care about you.

I really feel good when my mom gives me a hug and says, "Have a nice day" before I leave the house. Some people might take a little thing like that for granted, but not me. Also, one day in a store I asked a salesclerk where to find something, and out of the blue she said, "You have a beautiful smile." For the rest of the day I was happy. These kinds of things have to come naturally and from the heart, but they make all the difference in the way a person feels.

Respect from my family and friends makes me feel the best. I don't care if I'm not the best football player, or don't get the highest grade on a test, or don't succeed at everything I do. I only care that I tried my best and people respect me for it.

If someone says something mean about you, but you don't mind that much because you know they're wrong—that means you have self-confidence.

In this unit, "Building Self-Confidence and Communication Skills," you'll learn how self-confidence affects our feelings about ourselves, our relationships with others, and our performance in and out of school. It may seem that everybody wants self-confidence, but only the lucky ones are born with it. However, we can increase our own self-confidence. The sessions in Unit 2 tell us how. You'll read about the three main ways to improve self-confidence:

- Recognizing and developing our own skills and abilities
- Feeling appreciated and appreciating others
- Being responsible for our behavior

During this unit we'll be looking at our skills and abilities and thinking about how we can improve them. One special skill we'll practice is effective listening, because listening can affect self-confidence. Good listeners increase their own self-confidence by having a valuable skill. They also increase the speaker's self-confidence by making him or her feel appreciated.

Being responsible includes learning how to make healthy decisions with the guidance of parents and other adults. In Unit 2 you'll practice six steps that will help you develop positive decision-making skills. This is another way to gain self-confidence.

The article and the story for this unit both focus on self-confidence. Rick Little, author of "You Can Do It If You Think You Can," believes that no matter who you are, you can build your own self-confidence. The short story for this unit, "A New Start," shows how self-confidence affects people's actions, the way they relate to other people, and the decisions they make.

GETTING STARTED

We are all more confident at some times than at others. List two situations in which you are usually confident. For example, when you sing in the choir, catch a fly ball, or take a quiz in your favorite class.

1. _____

2. _____

Now list two situations in which you wish you were more confident. These might be situations you try to avoid because they make you uncomfortable. (We'll come back to this list later.)

1. _____

2. _____

UNIT PROJECTS

Complete at least one unit project by working on your own, with a partner, or with the class.

1. Ask family members to write short descriptions of happy childhood memories on slips of paper. Put the slips in a jar. As a slip is pulled out and read, the family guesses whose it is. The person then tells more about that memory while the family listens. Describe what you learned in a report.

2. Meet one new person each week during the next month. Try to get to know people of all ages—children, peers, adults, and elderly people. Practice giving your full attention and using your other listening skills. Describe your experiences in a report. What did you learn? How did your communication skills help?

3. Gather family members together and ask one person at a time to sit in an "appreciation chair." Have the family tell the person all the things they like and respect about that person. Give everyone a turn. Write a report about the activity, making sure not to share anything that might embarrass family members.

4. Do something for someone else. Be a good listener for someone in need, visit an elderly friend, mow a neighbor's lawn, do someone's grocery shopping, take care of a child, run an errand, fix something that's broken, make someone dinner or a cake, and so on. Write a one-page report explaining what you did and what you learned.

5. Write a rap about being a good listener. Describe the steps to good listening and tell how to use them every day. Also explain why good listening is important to both the speaker and the listener. Perform your rap for the class.

THREE-LEGGED STOOL OF SELF-CONFIDENCE

NAME: _____ DATE: _____

• •

Complete the following self-inventory.

1. Three things I do well:

_____

_____

_____

2. Three things other people appreciate about me:

_____

_____

_____

3. Three ways I show I'm responsible at home or at school:

_____

_____

_____

*Who can say more than
this rich praise, that you
alone are you?*

—**William Shakespeare**

37

BOUNDARY BREAKERS

NAME: _____ DATE: _____

• •

Write your responses to these topics.

Two people (living or dead) I'd like to talk with and the reasons why:

1. _____

_____

2. _____

_____

Two things I'd change if I were President of the United States or Prime Minister of Canada and the reasons why:

1. _____

_____

2. _____

_____

Two other periods in time I'd like to live in and the reasons why:

1. _____

_____

2. _____

_____

Two places I'd like to visit and the reasons why:

1. _____

_____

2. _____

_____

Two things I'd like to learn how to do and the reasons why:

1. _____

_____

2. _____

_____

KEYS TO LISTENING

Read the following information carefully.

FOCUS YOUR ATTENTION.

Make the speaker the center of your attention. Nod or lean toward the speaker. Maintain a comfortable level of eye contact. Be sure not to read or look around the room while the speaker is talking.

TUNE IN TO UNDERSTAND.

Listen so you clearly understand the speaker's point of view. Do not interrupt to tell your own stories, give your opinion, or offer un-asked-for advice. Listen not only for *what* is being said, but also for *how* it is being said. Then restate the speaker's ideas and feelings. For example, "That sounds very frustrating for you." Restating helps make sure you really do understand the meaning behind the words.

ASK FOR MORE INFORMATION, OPINIONS, AND FEELINGS.

Without interrupting, encourage the speaker to tell you more by asking questions about why, where, or how something happened. For example, "What else did you try?" Offer comments such as "I bet you'll have a great time!" or "That's too bad!" Also ask for opinions and feelings to make sure you understand what the speaker is saying.

A man has two ears and one mouth that he hear much and speak little.
—German proverb

LOOKING AT LISTENING

NAME: _____ DATE: _____

· ·

Check the things you did during this session.

_____ 1. I focused my attention.

_____ 2. I used a comfortable level of eye contact.

_____ 3. I showed I was listening by these actions:

_____

_____

_____

_____ 4. I didn't interrupt.

_____ 5. I asked for more information, opinions, and feelings.

_____ 6. I summarized what my partners said.

_____ 7. I showed respect for my partners' opinions by these actions:

_____

_____

_____

_____ 8. I did not take more than my share of the time.

He who listens, understands.

—West African proverb

YOU CAN DO IT
IF YOU THINK YOU CAN

BY RICK LITTLE

I'll never be good enough for the team. I'm not going to try out.

My brother and sister are always chosen for everything, and they get much better grades in school than I do. Sometimes I think my parents really love them more than me.

I don't like the way my braces look. I'm not going to smile again until these things come off!

What if I don't do well on the test? I have to get a B in this class or my parents will ground me for weeks.

Ever feel this way—like you just aren't good enough to meet everybody's expectations? You're not alone.

If you've sometimes felt unwanted or if you think maybe everybody else is better than you are, here's some good news. There are plenty of ways you can discover your hidden talents and gifts. You can learn how to feel better about yourself—if you're ready to try.

HOW WOULD YOU RATE YOURSELF?

What would you say if I asked you to rate your self-confidence on a scale of one to ten? Would you be a super-confident "ten," a down-in-the-dumps "one," or somewhere in between?

Your answer might depend on what's happened to you during the day. But are you basically happy with yourself? Are you a confident person? Or do you always think of others as being better and having more than you? Experts tell us that people who have built their self-confidence do better in school, get better grades, have more friends, have a better chance of getting the kind of job they want, and are more likely to have a rewarding and fulfilling future.

Self-confidence affects our attitudes and performance. When we feel self-confident, we find something positive in each new experience. But when we don't feel so confident, every setback just seems to bring us down even more.

Your attitudes, in turn, have a lot to do with your ability to succeed and be happy. Even though you can't see them, your attitudes are as much a part of you as your arms and legs. They show the world how you feel deep down about yourself and your life. And they affect the way your life is going to turn out.

YOU CAN MAKE A DIFFERENCE

In my own life I've had some tough times. Like a lot of other people, my family has had its share of problems. I had the constant feeling when I was a kid of not being good enough, of not being able to help myself and my family get through our problems. Sometimes I felt like giving up. But then I discovered something. Once I decided to stop looking at everything that was going wrong in my life (this wasn't always easy), I slowly began to notice the good things. Then I

began to reach out to help other people with their problems. It seemed as though the more I was willing to reach out to others, the less serious my own problems seemed.

I found as time went on that self-confidence is like a stool supported by three legs. Each one of the legs is important. Take away one of the legs, and the stool will collapse. The three legs of self-confidence are:

- Being responsible
- Having skills
- Feeling appreciated

Self-confident people have all three of these legs supporting them, whether they think about it or not. Let's look at each one of these three legs of self-confidence. They can make all the difference.

BEING RESPONSIBLE

Have you ever heard comments like these?

Why do I keep getting into trouble? Everything always seems to go wrong for me.

I'll never win. I'm just not a lucky person.

I won't ever get a good grade in that class because the teacher doesn't like me.

I think I've said all these things at one time or another. Sometimes we say things like this when we don't want to accept responsibility for what happens to us. It's always somebody else's fault, somebody else's responsibility. So we go into situations with the feeling that we don't have any power. We feel helpless.

Of course, we can't change everything that's going on around us. We can't control the weather or what time the school bus arrives. But that doesn't mean we're helpless. Far from it!

I've found that you can develop a positive attitude by looking at every part of your life and seeing the difference between those things that you can control and those things that you can't control. For example, I couldn't control the fact that my family was having problems, but I could control how I expressed my anger. Instead of yelling at my parents or getting mad, I could choose more positive ways to express myself.

If you have a positive attitude, you look for ways to solve problems that you can solve, and you let go of the things you can't control.

Sure, you'll still have some problems, even when you're trying hard to have a positive attitude. Sometimes you'll fail, even when you're thinking positively. Everyone fails at something once in a while. The important thing is how you react to failure. You can either dwell upon your failures or problems, or you can turn your problems into possibilities.

Several years ago I met Danielle, a positive, optimistic young girl who seemed to know exactly what she wanted in life. She was a talented pianist and hoped to play with a major orchestra some day. Then she was in a car crash.

When I visited Danielle recently, everything had changed. Although her hands *look* fine, nerve damage prevents her from playing the piano the way she once did. Her dream has been shattered, and so has her positive attitude. She has given up.

Danielle reminded me of someone else I'd met, named Tanisha. She too had been in a bad car crash, one that changed her life by creating lasting medical problems. But there was something very different about Tanisha—a sparkle, a warm smile, an attitude of confidence.

After her accident Tanisha had started a program to help other people who have been injured. What was different about her? She had "turned her scars into stars." She knew she couldn't change what had happened to her. But she could choose to live the rest of her life in love, not anger.

You can develop a positive attitude by recognizing that there will be both good and bad in your life and then deciding to emphasize the good. When you do this, the good in your life increases. Why is this true? Because goodness attracts goodness. In a similar way, people with a positive attitude attract others to them.

Recently, when I described the idea of being responsible and having a positive attitude to a group of students, a girl named Elena came up to me after the meeting.

"When you started to talk about responsibility, I thought of a time in my life when I didn't want to accept responsibility for anything," Elena said. "It was one of the most unhappy times of my life. I don't know why, but I just felt like I had no control over anything. Part of the problem was that I was feeling very unsure of myself.

"I started going around with a group of kids who were always in trouble. I guess all of us were feeling unsure, but nobody admitted it. Some of the kids were using drugs, so I had to prove how cool I was and use them too. I started staying out late, not doing my homework, and arguing with my parents a lot. And if they tried to talk with me about what was wrong, I'd tell them they didn't understand me. But I didn't feel that the kids I hung around with understood me either. Most of them just listened to music all the time and didn't talk much.

"I was really headed downhill until an old friend visited from Toronto—we used to be best friends, but she moved away a couple of years ago. We could talk about anything. I really trusted her. But she took one look at me and said, 'Elena, what is wrong with you? You've changed so much, and I don't like it!' She really told me the truth about myself. I realized I had stopped taking responsibility for my life. I was letting that group of kids make all my important decisions. But I knew they didn't really care about me at all."

The "three-legged stool" is adapted from Jim Fay's *Discipline With Love and Logic*. Evergreen, CO: Cline-Fay Institute, Inc. 1982.

What would you have done if you'd been in Elena's situation? How would you have felt if an old friend told you some truths about yourself that you didn't want to hear?

Elena decided to take control of her life again. She realized she needed to make some positive changes. She began by dropping her "troublemaker" friends. She worked a lot harder in school, and soon her grades improved greatly. She joined some after-school clubs and began to meet new friends. By the time she told me this story, her whole attitude toward herself had changed. She'd decided she could accept responsibility—and make a difference in her life.

Elena showed a great deal of courage. But you don't have to wait for someone else to tell you the truth. You can decide for yourself that it's time to turn your life around and accept responsibility for your own behavior.

HAVING SKILLS

The second supporting leg of self-confidence is being good at something. We don't have to succeed at everything we try, but it's a great confidence-builder to know we have some special skills.

A friend of mine named Julio once told me about an important time in his life when having a special skill made a big difference in his self-confidence. Here is his story.

Julio wasn't having one of his better days. Just as he was about to leave for school, he found out his bike had a flat tire. So instead of riding to school, he had to run. His lunch fell out of his backpack while he was rushing down the street, and it landed right in a puddle. And he hadn't even gotten to school yet!

Julio was still feeling pretty bad when he got to his first class. At least it was math, his favorite subject. As usual the teacher started out by reviewing the previous day's homework. She said that only one person in the class had gotten the correct answer to the last problem. Julio was startled when the teacher called on him to tell how he'd handled it. To his surprise, he was the one—the only one in the class—with the right answer. "Julio, you did a great job of figuring out how to solve a very difficult problem!" the teacher said. For the rest of the day Julio felt full of confidence.

Have you ever felt that way yourself?

"Julio must be really good at math," you might be saying. "I'm not really good at anything." Again, I can tell you that your attitude is the key. You may not be the very best athlete or student, but you have your own talents and skills. Maybe you're a good speller, a good baseball pitcher, or a good artist. Maybe you like to make model airplanes or play the piano. Maybe you're a really good listener and a lot of your friends talk to you about their problems. You don't have to be the *best*—just skillful at something.

You can develop special skills of some kind if you work at it. It's a matter of really trying and not giving up. Very few people are good at something the first time they try it. (Or even the second or third time!)

Whatever you do, whatever you're good at, knowing you can do certain things well is a basic building block of self-confidence. Remember, no one has exactly the same gifts, skills, and ideas you have. You are the best "you" there is.

FEELING APPRECIATED

For me, feeling appreciated—loved, liked, respected, listened to, accepted—can make everything that happens in life so much better. We gain self-confidence when we feel accepted and loved.

Feeling loved from the earliest moments of childhood helps us to appreciate others, but the ability to appreciate others and be appreciated in return is something we can learn. We don't have to be born with it. Appreciation is like sunshine—it brings joy to everyone who comes in contact with it. A 14-year-old boy named Darryl told me a story that says a great deal about how important it is to feel appreciated:

Whatever you do, whatever you're good at, knowing you can do certain things well is a basic building block of self-confidence.

When Darryl was in grade seven, he was transferred to a new school because he had caused problems in his old one. He wanted to change his behavior and get back on track, but a few kids in his new school found out why he had transferred. They told others, and soon Darryl was having trouble making friends. He had no one to sit with at lunch. He was the last one picked for a soccer team in gym class.

Then one day when Darryl was walking home from the bus stop, another boy who rode his bus challenged him to a race. Darryl lost, but he didn't mind. The other boy, Jared, asked if Darryl wanted to meet later to shoot some baskets. They spent the whole afternoon playing basketball and just having a good time together. "The next day at lunch," Darryl told me, "Jared invited me to sit with him and his friends. He told everyone I was really good at hook shots. And I knew he meant it. And I knew he didn't care what kind of trouble I had gotten into before. That made me feel really good, as though I could start fresh, make new friends, and succeed this time."

Darryl learned the importance of feeling appreciated for who and what you are.

Everyone needs the assurance that someone loves and accepts us just the way we are.

Who in your life makes you feel that way?

Remember that showing appreciation is like planting seeds. The more you sow, the more you'll get back in return.

YOU CAN MAKE IT HAPPEN

At this point you may be thinking, "All this stuff is okay for people who are self-confident to begin with. But what about people who have never felt very skillful, appreciated, or responsible? It's not easy to change negative thoughts about yourself."

But you can! Here are a few ideas to help you develop your own self-confidence:

Focus on the things you enjoy and do well. Could you do these things better with a little extra work and practice? If so, take the time. You'll feel better not just about your skills, but about yourself.

Focus on what's good and special about yourself, and you'll begin to like yourself a lot more. Young people tend to be very self-critical—always checking how they look and wishing they looked like someone else. Try focusing on your best qualities, physical and otherwise.

Look for new ways to be more responsible. Maybe you can lend a hand with cooking or cleaning up after meals. Perhaps you can volunteer to read to a young child or help a neighbor with painting or repairing something. You might even talk to your family about finding a part-time job. Volunteer for special tasks and assignments in school. Make the extra effort. You'll feel good about yourself, and people will appreciate your help.

Believe in yourself, and you'll be on your way to great success. Remember that your attitude is one of the keys to self-confidence.

Help others develop their self-confidence. Believe it or not, this is one of the most effective ways you can build your own confidence. Listen to people, appreciate them, and include them in your group. Don't laugh when other kids say mean things to them or call them names. Help them feel capable and responsible. You'll soon discover that by helping others become stronger, you'll become stronger, too. Give freely of praise, appreciation, respect, honesty, caring, and concern. As you share these gifts, they'll keep coming back to you. They'll help make you the person you really want to be.

. . . .

FACTUAL QUESTIONS:

1. Rick Little tells about an important discovery he made. What was it?

   _____

2. According to the author, what three things are necessary for self-confidence?

   _____

   _____

3. Why does Rick Little think a person's attitude is so important in building self-confidence?

   _____

4. What are two examples of "becoming more responsible"?

   _____

5. In what way was Elena courageous?

   _____

6. According to the article, how can we strengthen our skills?

   _____

   _____

7. What are three of the ways Rick Little says you can gain self-confidence?

   _____

INTERPRETIVE QUESTIONS:

8. What are some reasons why someone might feel like giving up after being in a serious automobile crash?

   _____

   _____

9. Why does Rick Little think it's important to understand which things in your life you can control and which things you can't?

   _____

   _____

10. What does the story of Elena tell you about self-confidence?

    _____

    _____

11. What did Julio discover about himself that made him feel self-confident?

    _____

    _____

12. What did Darryl learn about self-confidence?

    _____

    _____

THINKING ABOUT RESPONSIBILITY

NAME: _____ DATE: _____

• •

Read your group's situation card and fill in the answers below.

1. What did the irresponsible person do? _____

_____

_____

2. What were the negative consequences?

   To the irresponsible person: _____

   _____

   To anyone else directly affected: _____

   _____

   To the family, school, or community: _____

   _____

3. What responsible behavior or action would have been more helpful in this situation? _____

   _____

   _____

4. What would have been the positive consequences of this action?

   To the responsible person: _____

   _____

   To anyone else directly affected: _____

   _____

   To the family, school, or community: _____

   _____

No snowflake in an avalanche ever feels responsible.

—**Stanislaw Jerzy Lee**

STEPPING UP TO GOOD DECISIONS

NAME: _____ DATE: _____

• •

Read these steps carefully.

Give me a fish and I will eat today. Teach me to fish and I will eat for a lifetime.

—**Chinese Proverb**

STEP SIX: RETHINK your decision. (How did things turn out? Should you decide differently next time?)

STEP FIVE: DO what you decided.

STEP FOUR: CHOOSE the best course of action.

STEP THREE: PREDICT the consequences of each positive option.

STEP TWO: THINK about the options. Throw out any options that could lead to trouble. If you're not sure, ask yourself:

❏ Is it against the law, rules, or the teachings of my religion?

❏ Is it harmful to me or to others?

❏ Would it disappoint my family or other important adults?

❏ Is it wrong to do? (Would I be sorry afterward?)

❏ Would I be hurt or upset if someone did this to me?

STEP ONE: IDENTIFY the decision to be made.

DECISIONS! DECISIONS!

NAME: _____ DATE: _____

Complete the steps below to practice making a positive decision.

STEP ONE: IDENTIFY the decision to be made.

_____

STEP TWO: THINK about the options. **Throw out any options that could lead to trouble. If you're not sure, ask yourself:**

- Is it against the law, rules, or the teachings of my religion?
- Is it harmful to me or to others?
- Would it disappoint my family or other important adults?
- Is it wrong to do? (Would I be sorry afterward?)
- Would I be hurt or upset if someone did this to me?

STEP THREE: PREDICT the consequences of each positive option.

Option 1: _____

Advantages: _____

_____

Disadvantages: _____

_____

Option 2: _____

Advantages: _____

_____

Disadvantages: _____

_____

Option 3: _____

Advantages: _____

_____

Disadvantages: _____

_____

STEP FOUR: CHOOSE the best course of action.

My choice: _____

STEP FIVE: DO what you decided.

STEP SIX: RETHINK your decision.

WHAT SHOULD YOU DO?

NAME: _____ DATE: _____

• •

Read the situation and then complete the steps below to practice making a positive decision. For help, refer to the *Decisions! Decisions!* worksheet you completed in class.

Ask a parent or another adult to help you complete this worksheet.

> You are baby-sitting your six-year-old brother. After you come home from the store, you notice he has a candy bar. He says he put it in his pocket at the store when no one was looking. What should you do?

STEP ONE: IDENTIFY the decision to be made.

_____

STEP TWO: THINK about the options. Refer to your *Will It Lead to Trouble?* card to reject any negative options. List several positive options.

Option 1: _____

_____

_____

Option 2: _____

_____

_____

Option 3: _____

_____

_____

STEP THREE: PREDICT what might happen for each positive option.

Option 1: _____

Advantages: _____

_____

Disadvantages: _____

_____

Option 2: _____

Advantages: _____

_____

Disadvantages: _____

_____

Option 3: _____

Advantages: _____

_____

Disadvantages: _____

_____

STEP FOUR: CHOOSE the best course of action.

Our choice: _____

Imagine you carried out the best course of action. What do you think the result would be? How would your brother react? How would you react? Describe what you think the consequences would be.

_____

_____

_____

A NEW START

José stopped just ahead of Rico and blocked the sidewalk with his bike. He was dressed the same as always: black jeans, black boots, and a black motorcycle jacket. José was only 13, but he was big for his age—and always mad about something.

As he walked home from school and looked around his neighborhood, Rico couldn't help thinking that his name was pretty funny. In Spanish *rico* means "rich," but his family was anything but rich.

Ahead of him was the house where his family had been living for the last two months. They would probably live there for another two years until his father finished school and they could return to their hometown a day's drive south.

The houses on the street stood on concrete blocks and looked as if they had all been made by the same giant cookie cutter. At least a coat of white paint made Rico's house look a little better than some of the others. Most of them had never been painted.

No, his family didn't have much money, but his father always said they were rich in family and friends, rich in knowledge, and rich in their love for each other. And his father was right.

Back home his father had been a respected teacher in the high school and had been elected to the school board. People said that with more schooling he would be a leader in their community—a man whose own parents were farm workers. It almost made Rico dizzy to think about it, how great his father's future was. But that was why they were here in the city. For Papa's future.

Just then a boy rode past Rico on his dirt bike. It was José, a kid his age from the neighborhood. José stopped just ahead of Rico and blocked the sidewalk with his bike. He was dressed the same as always: black jeans, black boots, and a black motorcycle jacket. José was only 13, but he was big for his age—and always mad about something.

"Hey, Rico! It looks like I'm in your way." José's voice was heavy with sarcasm. "I am *so* sorry."

Rico walked out into the street to get around José. He looked José straight in the eye but didn't say a word.

José turned on his bicycle seat and called after him. "Rico, you got a problem. You got a serious problem. You talk too much."

Rico climbed the front steps of his house, walked slowly across the sagging porch, and went inside. He never said anything, and he never looked back. But he knew he would have to do something about the situation soon. It was getting worse all the time.

Later that afternoon, Rico and his little brother Pepe walked to a field near their house. It was a big vacant lot where the city had torn down a row of old houses. For now it belonged to the kids. The boys climbed through the hole in the fence that surrounded the field. Rico was glad to see they had the place to themselves.

"Let's do pop-ups," Rico said. "Get ready. Here it comes." Pepe ran out into the middle of the field and caught the ball right in the pocket of his glove.

"All right!" Rico yelled in the same kind voice his father used when they played catch together. "Now you pop me one."

The younger boy hurled the softball wildly, and it went rolling off into a clump of weeds.

"I'm sorry!" Pepe said.

Rico chased after it. "It's okay. You're getting better. Just try to put your whole body into it." Without breaking his stride, Rico scooped up the ball and turned to throw another one to Pepe.

Then he stopped dead. José was standing just inside the fence opening.

Even from across the field José sounded mean and sarcastic. "Lookin' like a champion, Rico. Let's see ya do your stuff."

"Go for it," Rico shouted to his brother, throwing another pop-up. Pepe ran after the ball but missed it.

"Aw, too bad," José said loudly.

"Throw it to me," Rico called. "Throw me a low one."

As he caught Pepe's ball, Rico saw José moving toward him. "Rico, we gotta talk," José said as he came closer. "We don't talk enough, you and me. If you talked to me, I might not want to beat you up."

"Talk to him, Rico," Pepe shouted from across the field. "Talk to him!"

"It's okay," he called. "I'll be all right."

"Sure," José said. "He'll be just fine. After I'm done with him, he won't be feeling a thing." By now José was standing so close Rico could feel his breath. José was at least three inches taller than Rico.

Rico tried to keep his body from shaking. He looked José straight in the eye. "I'm not afraid of you."

José looked at the ground for a moment as if he were thinking. Then suddenly he flipped his head up. "Well, we gotta do something about that, don't we?"

Before Rico knew what was happening, José had grabbed his shirt by the collar and pulled him forward. "We just gotta do something about that."

José drew his arm back, but Rico ducked just as he swung his fist. In the same motion Rico bent forward and butted his head into José's stomach. José let out a yelp of surprise. Before José had time to recover, Rico shoved him off balance. In a moment José was lying flat on his back, and Rico was on top of him, pinning his shoulders.

José struggled but couldn't force Rico off. He glared up at Rico, his coal eyes blazing.

The fight had lasted less than a minute, but Rico knew it was over. He stood up, brushed the dirt off his hands, and reached for his mitt lying on the ground. Now he felt very calm. "No hard feelings, José."

José dusted off his jacket and pants as he stood up. "You make me sick! I won't forget this. You watch out."

Rico said nothing. He stood watching until José disappeared through the hole in the fence.

Later that evening just before dinner, the whole family said their prayers together, as usual. Then everybody got a chance to share something about the day.

"Pepe, why are you so quiet tonight?" Papa asked. "Nothing happened to you today?"

"Rico may not be so big, but he's strong," Pepe blurted out. Then he looked quickly toward his brother.

"That's very interesting," Papa said. "Anything else?"

"No, Papa, I promised Rico I wouldn't tell."

Everyone looked at Rico—Mama, Papa, Pepe, Elida, Carmen, and Rita—waiting for him to speak.

"José tried to beat me up," Rico finally said with a sigh. "So I pinned him on the ground. It was no big deal."

"Oooh, I don't like that boy!" his older sister Carmen said. "He's trouble."

"Maybe we don't know the whole story," said Papa. "José *does* have some problems at home."

"Yes," said Mama. "His mama is very sick, and his father's not with him. That's not his fault."

"His mama drinks too much," offered Elida, the oldest child. "Once I smelled one of the bottles she threw out. Phew!"

"I was thinking," Mama said slowly. "Maybe José thinks no one cares about him. That could make anyone mean."

> **"Maybe we don't know the whole story," said Papa. "José does have some problems at home."**

The whole family was quiet for a minute. Then Pepe asked in a hushed voice, "What do you think José will do to Rico?"

Papa shook his head. "If anything happens, José will be hearing from me. Now let's eat."

For the next several days, Rico saw nothing of José. Then one evening after supper Mama sent him to the corner store to buy milk for breakfast. Pepe tagged along.

The brothers were walking toward the dairy section at the back of the store when Pepe gasped and grabbed Rico's arm. "There's José!" he whispered.

Sure enough, José had come into the store behind them. They watched as he walked over to the candy display. He picked up a candy bar, looked at it closely, and tossed it back on the shelf. Then he picked up a different kind, looked it over, and tossed it back, too.

Rico and Pepe stayed out of sight as José sauntered down the aisle to the rack of magazines and comic books. He hadn't seen them yet.

Rico didn't want to hide from José, but there was no use in asking for trouble. He and Pepe quietly headed down a different aisle toward the dairy section, trying not to attract José's attention.

"Hey, you!" called a loud voice in the next aisle.

Pepe jumped and grabbed Rico again, but Rico whispered, "That's not José. I know his voice."

"This isn't the liberry, you know," the voice said. "If you wanna read that, you gotta pay for it!"

Rico looked cautiously around the corner of the aisle. The store clerk was standing a few feet from José with his hands on his hips. He was about eighteen, but no taller or heavier than José.

"Get lost," José mumbled without looking at the clerk. He put one comic book back and picked up another one.

"What did you say?" the clerk demanded.

José opened the comic book and started to look through it. The clerk's face was getting redder and redder. Other customers were gathering to watch.

"You know, I saw you standing by the candy a few minutes ago," the clerk spit out. "I bet you stole something!"

Finally José turned and looked at the clerk. "Oh, yeah? Then where is it?"

The clerk looked at José's hands holding the comic book. Then he glanced down at the pockets in José's pants. They were completely flat. "I bet you stuffed it in your jacket."

"Well . . ." José put down the comic book and held out his arms. "Why don't you come over here and look for it?"

"The manager will do that!" the clerk snarled. He practically ran to the back of the store to get her.

"Good!" Pepe whispered. "José deserves to get in trouble!"

"But he didn't steal any candy," Rico said softly. "We were watching him. I'm sure he didn't."

Rico thought of leaving right then, but they hadn't bought the milk yet. And now Pepe was tugging on his sleeve.

"That lady—Mama knows her!" he whispered loudly, pointing to the manager who was walking with the clerk toward José. "She talks to Mama all the time when we come in here."

But now she was talking to José. "What's going on here? My clerk says you stole some candy. Let's empty those pockets."

José emptied out the pockets of his jacket. "I didn't steal nothing!"

"You must have ate it already!" the clerk said.

"Then where is the wrapper?" José asked. "Do you think I ate that, too?"

"Hey, no reason to get smart, kid!" the manager said. She looked around at the other customers. "Did anyone else see what happened?"

Rico took a step backward. Should he stick up for José, after José had threatened to beat him up? After José had already *tried* to beat him up?

Or should he keep his mouth shut because José was such a bully? Maybe Pepe was right. Maybe José *did* deserve anything he got.

Rico glanced down. Pepe was looking up at him, waiting for him to decide. Then Rico remembered what Papa had said: "Maybe we don't know the whole story."

And Mama: "Maybe José thinks no one cares about him." José sure needed someone to care about him now.

Rico walked around the end of the aisle until he faced José. José's eyes widened in surprise. Then he frowned and crossed his arms over his chest.

"José expects me to back up the clerk's story," Rico thought. José was in for another surprise.

"He didn't take any candy, ma'am," Rico said. "We—my brother and I— were watching and he put it all back."

José's mouth fell open, but the clerk squinted at Rico. "Oh, yeah? Well, let's check *your* pockets. I bet you're in this with him!"

Rico's mouth went dry. He knew he didn't have any candy in his pockets, but maybe he was in trouble, too. What would his parents say about this?

The manager looked at Rico and Pepe. Then she smiled. "Hey, aren't you the Rodríguez kids?"

Should he stick up for José, after José had threatened to beat him up?

Or should he keep his mouth shut because José was such a bully?

"See, I told you Mama knows her!" Pepe blurted to Rico. "Me and Mama, we come in here all the time and she always talks to you," he said to the clerk.

"I thought so," said the manager. She quietly looked at the clerk, José, and Rico in turn. She turned back to the clerk. "I don't see any evidence that either one of these boys took anything. Now get back to work! We've got customers waiting."

Then she winked at Pepe. "Tell your Mama I look forward to talking to her soon!" she said, heading to the back of the store again.

The red-faced clerk hurried to the front of the store where a line of impatient customers waited for him. The rest of the stragglers drifted away, leaving José, Rico, and Pepe standing together.

José stared at the floor. "You didn't have to do that, Rico. I can take care of myself."

"Yeah, I could see that."

"What I mean is. . . ." José swallowed. "Uhh . . . thanks, man." Then he looked at Rico and smiled a little. "Hey, if you ever get in trouble, just call me, okay? I'll help you out."

Rico grinned. "I'll do that, if you promise not to beat me up afterward."

For a second, José seemed embarrassed.

"Oh, I guess I don't need to beat you up anymore." José grinned and looked down at Pepe. "But your little brother, he really needs some practice catching pop-ups. Maybe we can play catch sometime."

Rico looked José in the eye. He thought he saw a friend in there. "Yeah, maybe we can."

• •

FACTUAL QUESTIONS:

1. Where do Rico and José live?

   _____

2. Why is Rico's family living there?

   _____

3. In what ways does Rico think his family is rich?

   _____

4. What does Rico's family think of José? Why?

   _____

5. What does Rico do at the end of the story to help José?

   _____

INTERPRETIVE QUESTIONS:

6. What are some of the main differences and similarities between Rico and José?

   _____

   _____

7. When José tried to start a fight with Rico, how else could Rico have reacted? What are some
   appropriate ways to respond to a situation like this?

   _____

   _____

8. Why do you think Rico doesn't want to talk to José? Why doesn't Rico want to fight José?

   _____

   _____

9. After so much anger and misunderstanding has passed between them, why does Rico speak up when
   José is in trouble? Why do you think José's attitude toward Rico changes after that?

   _____

   _____

• •

10. Who in the story is a good listener? What does the story tell you about people listening to each other?

_____

_____

11. In what ways is José's three-legged stool of self-confidence fairly strong? In what ways is it weak? What could he do to gain more self-confidence?

_____

_____

12. During the story, what does José learn? What does Rico learn?

_____

_____

BUILDING SELF-CONFIDENCE

NAME: _____ DATE: _____

Answer the following questions. Then circle one of your answers in each section and follow through with it.

1. What are some ways you can build your own self-confidence?

_____

_____

_____

_____

_____

_____

2. What are some ways you can help build the self-confidence of others?

_____

_____

_____

_____

_____

If you have no confidence in yourself,
you are twice defeated in the race of life.
With confidence, you have won even
before you have started.

—**Marcus Garvey**

Looking Back

NAME: _____ DATE: _____

Look back at the situations you listed at the beginning of the unit. Remember the ones in which you wished you were more confident? Write them again below. Then explain two or three things you could do to gain confidence in each situation.

Situation 1: _____

Ways I could help myself become more confident in this situation:

_____

_____

_____

_____

_____

_____

_____

_____

_____

Situation 2: _____

Ways I could help myself become more confident in this situation:

_____

_____

_____

_____

_____

_____

_____

_____

_____

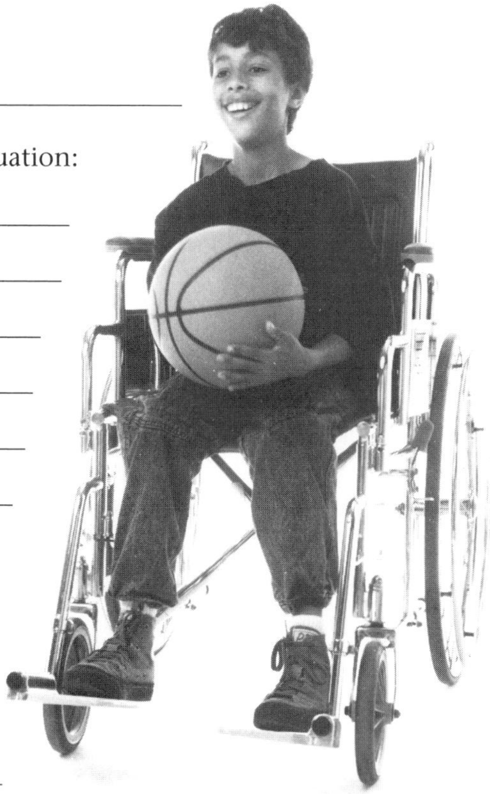

SERVICE PROJECT IDEAS

NAME: _____ DATE: _____

· ·

IN SCHOOL

Need: To help make school a positive place for everyone

Possible projects:

- Create posters with positive messages on friendship, cooperation, crosscultural understanding, school spirit, and other topics.
- Start a school-wide "Say Something Nice" campaign to eliminate put-downs. Make posters, read announcements over the P.A., and involve school staff.
- Begin an "Excellence in Education" campaign with posters, buttons, and bulletin boards encouraging students to strive to get good grades. Develop special awards.
- Plan an "Appreciation Day" for school staff.

Need: To beautify our school

Possible projects:

- Conduct a school cleanup campaign.
- Plant flowers and trees around the school.
- Design a hallway mural about the school's history.
- Sponsor a "Keep Our School Beautiful" campaign.
- Paint a hallway or a wall in the cafeteria.

IN THE COMMUNITY

Need: To help senior citizens

Possible projects:

- Write letters to people confined to their homes.
- Adopt a "grandparent" in the community.
- Plan a holiday dinner for senior citizens at a nursing home.
- Invite senior citizens to school for a special day of sharing and discussion.
- Create handmade gifts for special occasions.
- Send handmade birthday cards to people 80 or over.

Need: To help young children

Possible projects:

- Plan a special party for children in day care.
- Present a puppet show in an elementary school.
- Teach simple craft projects to children.
- Read stories to children in elementary school.
- Help with baby-sitting for special parent and community meetings.

Need: To help the homeless

Possible projects:

- Help organize a walk-, run-, or bike-athon to raise funds for a community shelter.
- Help cook or serve meals at a community soup kitchen.
- Collect food, clothing, and toys for distribution at local shelters.
- Learn about the local situation and write letters to local officials about the problems of the homeless.

MY SERVICE PROJECT IDEA

Need:

_____

_____

_____

_____

Possible Projects:

_____

_____

_____

_____

_____

_____

_____

_____

_____

_____

_____

_____

_____

_____

SERVICE PROJECT SURVEY

NAME: _____ DATE: _____

● ●

Write the four needs the class identified. Then ask family members and others to complete the survey.

Our Lions-Quest *Skills for Adolescence* class is planning a service project for the community or school. We have identified four major needs our class could address. Please indicate the one you think is the most worthwhile. We would also like to hear your ideas for possible projects.

Thank you for your help! We hope our project will help people in our school and our community.

1. _____

2. _____

3. _____

4. _____

RESPONDENT 1   **Need #:** _____

Project ideas:_____

_____

_____

_____

RESPONDENT 2   **Need #:** _____

Project ideas:_____

_____

_____

_____

RESPONDENT 3   **Need #:** _____

Project ideas:_____

_____

_____

_____

RESPONDENT 4   **Need #:** _____

Project ideas:_____

_____

_____

_____

When spider webs are woven together, they can tie up a lion. —**Ethiopian proverb**

CHOOSING A SERVICE PROJECT

NAME: _____ DATE: _____

Write your group's assigned need below. Then discuss the questions with your group and fill in your answers.

Need: _____

1. What are some reasons this is an important need for the class to address?

   _____

   _____

   _____

2. What is one short-term project the class could do to address this need?

   _____

   _____

3. What will be required to do this project? (Think about expenses, materials, adult help, transportation.)

   _____

   _____

   _____

4. What might keep this project from being successful?

   _____

   _____

   _____

5. What are *two* long-term projects the class might carry out to address this need?

   _____

   _____

   _____

   _____

One of the signs of passing youth is the birth of a sense of fellowship with other human beings as we take our place among them.

—Virginia Woolf

65

MAKING IT HAPPEN

SERVICE PROJECT PLAN

NAME: _____ DATE: _____

· ·

To plan your first service learning project, complete this worksheet.

1. The need we chose: _____
   _____

2. A brief description of our project: _____
   _____
   _____
   _____

3. Our project goals: _____
   _____
   _____
   _____
   _____

4. My committee: _____

JOBS TO BE DONE	WHO WILL DO THEM?	DEADLINE
_____	_____	_____
_____	_____	_____
_____	_____	_____
_____	_____	_____
_____	_____	_____
_____	_____	_____
_____	_____	_____
_____	_____	_____
_____	_____	_____

The distance is nothing; it is only the first step that is difficult.

—**Marquise du Deffand**

REVIEWING THE PROJECT IN CLASS

NAME: _____ DATE: _____

• •

Answer the following questions.

1. What skills did the class use to carry out this project?

_____

_____

_____

_____

2. What were the positive results?

_____

_____

_____

_____

3. What can we do to improve our next project?

_____

_____

_____

_____

The creation of a thousand forests is in one acorn. —**Ralph Waldo Emerson**

REVIEWING THE PROJECT WITH MY FAMILY

NAME: _____ DATE: _____

• •

Explain our service learning project to your family and ask an adult at home to answer these questions.

1. What is your understanding of the *Skills for Adolescence* service learning project? What did the class do?

_____

_____

_____

_____

_____

_____

_____

2. How did your child contribute to the project?

_____

_____

_____

_____

_____

_____

3. What do you think your child has learned or experienced as a result of working on this project?

_____

_____

_____

_____

_____

_____

_____

In all things that are purely social we can be as separate as the fingers, yet one as the hand in all things essential to mutual progress.

—Booker T. Washington

Project Notes

UNIT 3
MANAGING EMOTIONS IN POSITIVE WAYS

If you ask young teenagers what they have the hardest time talking about, they'll probably say "my feelings." Why are feelings so difficult to deal with? Why do they sometimes change from one hour to the next for no apparent reason?

Adolescence is a time of changing emotions. There's a good chance you're experiencing a wider range of feelings than ever before in your life. Listen to what a number of junior high and middle school students told us:

My friends understand my problems, and they can help. I think it's because they have the same problems. We actually have fun discussing them. But the only person who can really work out my problems is me.

A lot of times my parents can tell how I'm feeling by the way I look, and they'll ask if they can help. They give me suggestions, and I feel a lot better. Everybody needs someone who cares. It makes you feel so much better.

Anger is a hard emotion to control. I have a bad temper, but I try as much as possible not to show it. That way, no one knows how angry I can get.

I know I need to get a handle on my jealousy. I don't like feeling jealous, and I don't like it when other people are jealous. I think that we all should be happy with what we have and be thankful we have it.

The feelings that bother me the most are when I'm feeling down or sad. I can't seem to bring myself out of my bad mood. I want to feel more cheerful.

The feelings I'm most afraid of are the ones I don't share with people.

I can tell my feelings to my best friend and she really understands. But if I want advice, I go to my mom.

Feelings! Sometimes it seems you're hit by different feelings all day long. This can be both exciting and confusing, but it's normal for people your age. The good news is that you can learn to get a handle on them.

This unit will help you identify and learn to manage your feelings. During the activities and discussions, you'll discover that all your feelings have been shared by others, including your classmates! We'll talk about how we affect each other's feelings and how we can change negative feelings into more positive ones.

You'll learn a positive way to let others know when you're angry or hurt. You'll also have a chance to practice making decisions without letting angry feelings take over.

In "Understanding and Handling Your Feelings," Gary R. Collins remembers his experiences as an adolescent. Today Gary Collins is a psychologist who helps young people and their families work out their problems. He realizes that he had a lot of the same problems himself when he was your age, and he offers some helpful tips for dealing with them.

The short story for this unit, "A Moving Experience," tells about a 12-year-old who has many feelings of confusion and frustration. He tries to ignore them, but he discovers they just don't go away by themselves.

GETTING STARTED

Read the quotes again. Write two reasons why having feelings is important to you. Then write two reasons why feelings can lead to problems sometimes.

Reasons why having feelings is important:

1. _____

2. _____

Reasons why feelings can lead to problems sometimes:

1. _____

2. _____

UNIT 3
UNIT PROJECTS

Complete at least one unit project by working on your own, with a partner, or with the class.

1. List ten ways to communicate caring or affection to a friend or relative who lives some distance away. Choose five of these ways and follow through on them, communicating with at least three different people. Then write a report describing what you did, what the results were, and what you learned. Include your original list of ten ways to communicate.

2. Collect pictures, songs, poems, raps, or other expressions of positive ways to communicate emotions and handle strong emotions. Present and explain your collection to the class.

3. Read a book or short story about a young person who is having trouble with emotions. Write a two-page report that describes the emotions and how the person learned to deal with them effectively.

4. Watch a TV show or movie about a young person who is having trouble with emotions. Write a two-page report that describes the emotions and how the person learned to deal with them constructively.

EMOTION CLOCK

NAME: _____ DATE: _____

• •

Follow along as someone in your group reads the story aloud. Stop at the blank spaces and discuss words you think would fit there. Write *your own* choice of words in the blanks.

At 6:45 am, the alarm went off beside Shelly's bed. She reached over and shut it off. Then she thought about the day ahead—a test in science, playing volleyball in gym class, pizza for lunch in the school cafeteria. She felt _____.

Shelly rolled out of bed and reached for her favorite sweatshirt. It was missing! Then she noticed her younger sister, still asleep in her own bed. Natalie was wearing her sweatshirt! Now she felt

_____.

"Mom!" Shelly yelled. "Natalie's got my sweatshirt on!"

"Find something else to wear, Shelly," her mom called up the stairs. "And hurry up! Your breakfast is ready."

Natalie always gets her own way, Shelly told herself. She felt _____ as she searched under her bed for her second-most-favorite sweatshirt.

By 8:00 Shelly was hurrying to the corner where she always met Mike. They walked to school together almost every day. He was there, waiting for her. Now she felt _____.

Mike had an intramural football game after school that day. He was the quarterback for the blue team. "Are you coming to watch?" he asked Shelly.

"Sure!" she told him. Then she looked at her watch. "The bell's going to ring in three minutes!" They could barely see the school way down the street. Now they both felt _____.

They just made it in time. At 8:15 Shelly was sitting in science class, trying to catch her breath. She looked at the test. I know this stuff, she thought. She felt _____.

At 10:30 Shelly was in gym class. The teacher picked her to be captain of one of the volleyball teams. She felt _____.

The game was really close. At the very end, she missed a spike and her team lost. On the way to the locker room, her teammates patted her on the back. "Don't feel bad, Shelly," they said, but she felt

_____.

At least the pizza was hot and cheesy when Shelly had lunch at 12:15. As she ate, though, she noticed Mike talking to Sabrina at another table. Now she felt _____.

In English class at 1:30, the teacher handed back the essays. Uh oh, Shelly thought. Six words on her essay were circled in red. That meant they were misspelled. She felt _____.

At 3:00, Shelly finished her last class and headed for the football field. She wanted to watch Mike play in the game, but then she remembered how he was laughing with Sabrina at lunchtime. She felt

_____.

At 6:30 Shelly and Natalie set the table while her dad made hamburgers. By the time her mom hurried in from work, dinner was ready. "Our team won the game today," Shelly told them. She felt

_____.

Shelly walked to her friend Christa's house after dinner and they shot baskets in her driveway. "You're good!" Christa told Shelly. "You should try out for the team." Shelly tried not to show it, but she felt

_____.

At 10:15, Shelly set her alarm for the next day. She also found her favorite sweatshirt and put it under her pillow. At least tomorrow morning, she told herself, I won't have any trouble finding this! As she drifted off to sleep, she felt _____.

Write Your Own Bucket Story

NAME: _____ DATE: _____

On another sheet of paper, write your own "Bucket Story." Include an equal number of positive and negative events in your character's day. The outline below may help, but you don't have to use it. Be sure to describe how your character reacts to each event.

1. Wake up.

2. Get dressed.

3. Meet friends on the way to school.

4. Arrive at first class.

5. Eat lunch with best friends.

6. Go to gym class.

7. Take part in after-school activity.

8. Get home.

9. Greet brother or sister arriving home from school.

10. Help with chores after dinner.

11. Do homework.

12. Watch TV.

PITS TO PEAKS

NAME: _____ DATE: _____

• •

List two situations young people often face on the *Situation* lines
below. Then list possible negative (pits) and positive (peaks)
thoughts, emotions, and actions for each.

SITUATION 1 _____

Thought _____   Thought _____

_____   _____

Emotion _____   Emotion _____

_____   _____

Action _____   Action _____

_____   _____

SITUATION 2 _____

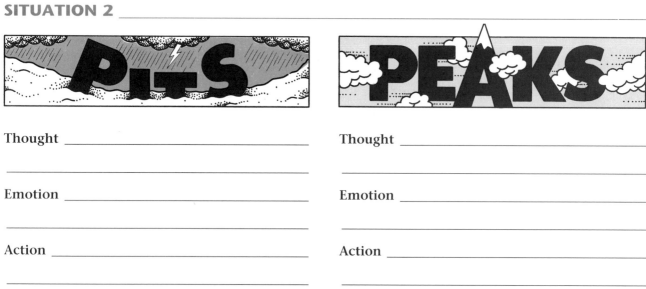

Thought _____   Thought _____

_____   _____

Emotion _____   Emotion _____

_____   _____

Action _____   Action _____

_____   _____

PITS TO PEAKS

UNIT 3

4-5 SESSION

NAME: _____ DATE: _____

• •

List two situations young people often face on the *Situation* lines below. Then list possible negative (pits) and positive (peaks) thoughts, emotions, and actions for each.

SITUATION 1 _____

PITS

Thought _____

_____

Emotion _____

_____

Action _____

_____

PEAKS

Thought _____

_____

Emotion _____

_____

Action _____

_____

SITUATION 2 _____

PITS

Thought _____

_____

Emotion _____

_____

Action _____

_____

PEAKS

Thought _____

_____

Emotion _____

_____

Action _____

_____

LEMONADE LEARNINGS

NAME: _____ DATE: _____

Read these positive statements and add one or more of your own.

The way I feel about myself doesn't depend only on others' opinions of me.

The only person who never makes a mistake is the person who never does anything.

I am special, the only one there is of me.

If I'm slower at some things than other people, that's just fine.

I will do what I can, with what I have, where I am.

I can't change others, but I can try to change myself.

I will try to see problems as opportunities.

I can't constantly depend on others; some things I have to do myself.

Instead of saying "if only I had," I will say "next time I will."

I can help other people, and I can ask for help when I need it.

I am prepared to lose once in a while.

I will be responsible for my own positive attitude.

I will try to live my life as an exclamation, not an explanation.

MY OWN POSITIVE STATEMENT:

_____

_____

*When life hands you lemons,
make lemonade!*

UNDERSTANDING AND HANDLING YOUR FEELINGS

BY GARY R. COLLINS

• •

Could you describe yourself in just a few words?

When I was your age, I would have picked three words to describe myself: stupid, ugly, and odd.

I thought I was stupid because it always seemed that the teacher asked me questions I couldn't answer. I used to wonder why everybody else in the class got the easy questions and "dumb old Gary" (that was me) got the hard ones. It wasn't long before I started to feel like a real klutz.

Maybe life would have been easier if I had been handsome, athletic, and well built, but I was overweight. I thought I was fat. I would try to slouch in my seat and hide from the teacher, but that was impossible because the girl who sat in front of me was skinny. Sometimes the other kids made comments about my size, and that didn't make me feel any better about myself. My mother thought I was beautiful. But what do mothers know about things like that? I thought I was ugly.

I also felt I was odd. As far as I knew, I was the only kid my age in the whole world who felt frustrated, criticized by others, and not smart enough to do much of anything, including answering questions.

What I didn't know then was that almost everybody feels stupid at times. Most of us—one expert says 95 percent of us—see things in ourselves that we don't like. Because of that, we get especially hurt inside when friends or brothers and sisters tease us and call us names. Even when people say nothing, it's easy to be discouraged because of the braces on your teeth, the zits that won't go away, or the fact that you seem to be a different size from everybody else in the whole school.

Feeling stupid, ugly, and odd is pretty common to young teenagers. It's also common—and normal—to feel angry, disappointed, rejected, sad, lonely, and guilty sometimes. And, as if that weren't enough, young teenagers often go through sudden and unexpected mood changes. You may feel happy one minute and sad the next, hardly even knowing why.

IT'S OKAY TO HAVE FEELINGS

When I was little, we were told that "big boys don't cry" and that nobody likes a "crybaby." Maybe you've heard this, too. Sometimes it seems that people think it's bad to express any kind of feelings, even happy ones.

After being warned for long enough not to express our feelings, most of us decide there must be something wrong with having feelings.

Let's begin, then, by reminding ourselves that everybody has emotions. It's impossible to be human and not have them. Because of feelings, our lives have variety and interest. If we didn't have

feelings, we would be like robots. We'd be blah, boring, mechanical, and not even able to understand what it means to have fun.

Emotions tend to seem especially intense when you're young. As you get older, the whole range of your feelings becomes more familiar. When you're young, though, it's easy to feel helpless and overwhelmed by emotions. When you start facing your feelings for the first time, things hit with greater force.

Let's suppose, for example, that you and your closest friend are going to be separated because of a family move. For a while it may seem that the loneliness and sadness will never go away.

Because your feelings are so strong, your reactions might be strong as well. Little irritations that might not bother an adult or even a younger child can plunge you into depression and worry. On the brighter side, adolescents have been known to do really crazy things to show their joy and happiness over something like a football victory that maybe isn't all that important. (This isn't a lot different from some adults who get really mad or who jump up and down and shout in excitement over a game on TV. But kids tend to do that kind of thing more freely and more often.)

You and I may not always like our feelings. Our emotions may make life miserable at times. Still, we need to admit that emotions are part of being human. If you try to deny your feelings, you're only kidding yourself.

EMOTIONS AFFECT OUR BODIES

Sometimes people call each other "scaredy-cat," but have you ever thought about this expression? When a cat is frightened, its heart starts beating faster, its muscles get tense, and there are changes in the chemicals in its bloodstream. Although the cat doesn't realize this, its body is getting ready for action. If the danger continues, the animal will do one of two things. It will defend itself, or it will run away as fast as it can.

Something like this also happens to people. When we are excited, angry, scared, or aroused by other emotions, our bodies go through many physical changes. Our hearts beat faster, and our muscles get tense. All of these changes make us more alert and ready to react. We, too, get ready to defend ourselves or run.

Human beings, however, have a problem that animals never face. If we give way to our feelings and let them take over, we can get into trouble. Have you ever said something in anger—or hit somebody— and regretted it later? Have you ever yelled at a teacher, told somebody you were lonely, or said you were in love, and then wished later you had kept your mouth shut? It isn't always wise to express your feelings freely.

Does this mean that it's smarter always to hide our feelings? No! If you keep feelings of anger, frustration, sadness, and bitterness hidden away or bottled up inside, your body stays tense. Physical illness can develop, and you can feel churned up inside. It can actually be bad for your health. (It isn't good to keep pleasant feelings inside either; all feelings need to be expressed.)

Feelings that you keep all bottled up inside don't just go away. It's as if you bought a bunch of bananas and stuck them in a cupboard. You might not be able to see them, but before long you'd smell them. And if you opened the cupboard, chances are you'd see little fruit flies hovering all over them. They'd be rotten.

You can try to treat emotions as if they were bananas in the cupboard. You can hide them and you can pretend they don't exist, but they'll still be around. And eventually you'll have to deal with them, just like those bananas.

SO WHAT DO WE DO WITH FEELINGS?

Sometimes feelings can make life more exciting; they can also make us miserable. Whenever feelings come along, then, we have to decide whether to let them out or hold them in—and to what degree.

Whenever feelings come along, then, we have to decide whether to let them out or hold them in—and to what degree.

Sometimes that decision can be easy. If your team is winning, you don't hesitate to shout wildly. But what if the team is losing and you feel like crying? How do you act when you're really angry at a friend, a teacher, a parent, or your brother? How do you act when the person who makes you most angry is yourself? What do you do when you're feeling disappointed, excited, lonely, or guilty?

The answers to these questions depend on two main things. First, where are you? Sometimes I cry if I'm really sad, but usually that only happens when I'm alone or with someone who accepts me and doesn't laugh. Crying at a funeral is appropriate. Crying in an ice cream store because they're all out of mint chocolate chip is not appropriate, unless you happen to be three years old. If you're at a football game, it's okay if you shout or laugh like crazy. But you'll get a little static if you do this while you're listening to a sermon in church.

How you show your feelings, therefore, depends on where you are.

How you show your feelings also depends on the kind of person you are.

Some people are expressive, while others like to play it cool and be self-controlled, at least in front of their friends. How, when, and where you express your emotions is a personal thing. A lot depends on your background, your culture, your family's way of expressing feelings, and what makes you feel comfortable. Everybody has feelings, but we express them in different ways.

HOW TO HANDLE YOUR FEELINGS

Can feelings be controlled? This is an important question—and the answer is yes. Feelings can almost always be handled.

I remember one time when I was part of my junior high school choir. We must have been pretty good because our choir was invited to sing in a big concert hall. We were competing with choirs from other schools for some sort of prize. Everybody was nervous; nobody wanted to make a mistake. When our turn came to sing, we filed up to the platform, stood up straight, and waited for the choir leader's signal to start singing. Everybody began at the same time.

Except me.

I made a mistake and started about half a second before everybody else. I really felt dumb, singing the first word all by myself in front of several thousand people. I can laugh about it now, but at the time I was really embarrassed and decided that we had lost the contest because of me. I kept thinking about it for weeks afterwards, and I had the feeling that everybody else in the choir remembered it just as vividly as I did. Maybe you've felt the same kind of embarrassment.

Feelings are like that. They often stay around and bother us for a long time. They drag us down and even affect the way we think. The first step in handling these emotions is to admit you have them. If you're mad, sad, glad, or having some other kind of feeling, admit it—at least to yourself.

Then think before you act. Do you remember the old idea that when you get mad you should count to ten before exploding? That isn't a bad suggestion. Sometimes a few seconds is all the time you need to stop yourself from saying something harmful or doing something you could be sorry for later.

Of course, it isn't always easy to control your feelings and actions. Have you ever worried about having to talk in front of the class or playing well in an important game? Maybe you were really anxious about what was going to happen, and then along came somebody who wanted to help. "It's okay," your friend may have said. "You don't have to worry about this."

Did that stop you from worrying? Absolutely not. Feelings don't go away just because you or somebody else decides that they should.

Some people are expressive, while others like to play it cool and be self-controlled, at least in front of their friends.

The best way to deal with feelings is to think about what caused them in the first place. Then we can try to do something about the causes. This leads me to another suggestion that may seem a little strange, but it works: talk to yourself about your feelings.

Lots of us talk to ourselves all the time. Usually we don't do it out loud because we don't want to look crazy and we don't want others to know what we're telling ourselves. When I was your age, I used to talk to myself about my lack of ability in sports. I have to confess that I'm a terrible athlete. That always made me feel inferior. A lot of kids in my school thought people who couldn't run fast or hit a baseball weren't worth much. At the time I pretty much talked myself into believing that this was true. Now I know that some people are good in athletics and some, like me, are better at other things. I guess I had to talk myself into believing that, too.

Not long ago I was watching a state track meet. When the starting gun sounded, one guy took off like a bullet and soon was ahead of everybody else in the race. The kids from his school cheered like crazy. He was a certain winner, even before the race was half over.

Then he tripped.

For some reason he lost his balance and fell flat on his face in the middle of the track. By the time he got to his feet and ran the rest of the distance, everybody else had crossed the finish line. It wasn't hard to see that this guy was disappointed, disgusted with himself, and fighting mad.

I don't know how he handled his feelings after the race. He could have spent the next few hours—or months—condemning himself, criticizing the "stupid track," and generally making himself and everybody else miserable.

Feelings are like that. Sometimes they take over our minds. But that doesn't have to happen. The runner could have asked himself several key questions. So could you in a similar situation:

- Why do I feel the way I do? (Because I made a mistake that caused me to fall in front of all those people, embarrassing me and letting down my school.)

- What can I do about it now? (Probably nothing, although it might help to talk to the track coach. He might have some suggestions to keep me from making the same mistake again.)

- Does my mistake mean I'm stupid and doomed to be a failure forever, or can I learn from it and move on? (Everybody makes mistakes, but you can learn from your experiences and do better next time.)

It's important to be honest with yourself in answering questions like these. Otherwise, the only person you're fooling is the most important person as far as your feelings are concerned—yourself.

The best way to deal with feelings is to think about what caused them in the first place. Then we can try to do something about the causes.

SOME OTHER TIPS ON HANDLING FEELINGS

Once you realize the importance of learning how to handle your feelings, you'll start to get into the habit. Next time you're struggling with some emotion, ask yourself the following two questions and try to come up with honest answers:

1. What is causing this feeling?
2. What can I do about it?

If you don't have any good answers, talk with a friend, parent, youth leader, counselor, coach, or teacher. When we're honest enough to share our feelings with another person, we've made an important step in handling how we feel. The sooner you learn this, the easier it will be to deal with your feelings.

Another important idea is to express your emotions without losing your cool. How do you do that? Tell others how you feel—honestly, but without ranting, raving, and making a fool of yourself. Sometimes it helps to not only tell someone how you feel, but why. Here are some examples:

- "When you take my things without asking, I feel really mad. Please ask me before using my stuff."
- "I feel really hurt when you walk away while I'm talking. I have something important to tell you and I wish you'd let me finish."

And if you sometimes forget all of this fine advice and blow your top, be quick to apologize. I'm a psychologist. People come to me to talk about their problems. So I'd like to be able to tell you that I always handle my emotions beautifully, that I never get discouraged, that I never yell at my kids, and that I'm a model of self-control. Well, don't believe it. Nobody can be perfect, and I'm no exception. At times all of us get carried away by our feelings, including me. The important thing is to be able to admit our mistakes and say we're sorry.

There's another thing you can do: don't let your mind make matters worse. A young friend of mine told me how he'd felt recently when he was rejected by some of the kids in his youth group. "We were pretty good friends for a while," he said, "but they kind of cooled off to me. Then they started ignoring me. I guess they decided I wasn't good enough for their group."

Did my friend sit around moping, thinking how awful he was, or planning how he could get revenge? No, he didn't. He admitted to himself that he felt hurt and sad because of what the other kids had done. Then he made up his mind to do two things. He would continue to be friendly to the people who were rejecting him. But he'd also get involved in other activities where he could find new friends. He didn't spend time brooding over his feelings so that matters got worse.

This brings us to one last suggestion for handling feelings: be willing to reach out to somebody else. Is there someone you know who is sad, discouraged, lonely, or feeling rejected? By taking a couple of minutes to encourage such people, you can really be a great help to them. What may surprise you is that this can make you feel pretty good as well. Some day you might find that another person will reach out to help you when you feel down.

Everybody has feelings. Emotions are an important part of being human. The more we recognize this—and understand our own and other people's feelings—the better off life will be for everybody.

FACTUAL QUESTIONS:

1. When Gary Collins was a teenager, what were some of the problems he faced?

_____

_____

2. What were some of the emotions he felt as a teenager? What triggered those emotions?

_____

_____

3. What emotions does he say are common to young teenagers?

_____

_____

4. How can emotions affect our bodies?

_____

_____

5. According to the author, how can our emotions get us into trouble?

_____

_____

6. Gary Collins mentions several things we can do to handle our emotions more effectively. What are they?

_____

_____

7. What two questions can we ask ourselves the next time we're struggling with an emotion?

_____

_____

INTERPRETIVE QUESTIONS:

8. The author tells us that emotions are okay. What does he mean by this?

_____

_____

9. What are some ways we can help others when they're feeling sad, discouraged, lonely, or rejected?

_____

_____

10. Why does Gary Collins think that everybody will benefit if each of us has a better understanding of our emotions and can express them in positive ways?

_____

_____

11. What does the author say about having a positive attitude toward possibly negative situations?

_____

_____

KEEPING COOL ABOUT GOOD DECISIONS

NAME: _____ DATE: _____

Complete this worksheet to determine the best course of action for your assigned situation.

KEEPING COOL WHEN YOU'RE NOT

Take a breath. (Calm down.)

Get a grip. (Name the emotion you need to control.)

Think it through. (Decide if you are ready to handle this situation in a positive way.)

Then, when you're ready:

STEP ONE: IDENTIFY the decision to be made. _____

STEP TWO: THINK about your options. **Throw out any options that can lead to trouble. Ask yourself:**

- Is it against the law, rules, or the teachings of my religion?
- Is it harmful to me or to others?
- Would it disappoint my family or other important adults?
- Is it wrong to do? (Would I be sorry afterward?)
- Would I be hurt or upset if someone did this to me?

STEP THREE: PREDICT what might happen for each positive option.

Option 1: _____

Advantages: _____

_____

Disadvantages: _____

_____

Option 2: _____

Advantages: _____

_____

Disadvantages: _____

_____

Option 3: _____

Advantages: _____

_____

Disadvantages: _____

STEP FOUR: CHOOSE the best course of action.

My choice: _____

STEP FIVE: DO what you decided.

STEP SIX: RETHINK your decision. (How did things turn out? Should you decide differently next time?)

A MOVING EXPERIENCE

"Andy, Mom and I have something to tell you," his father began. Then he stopped and cleared his throat.

Darn, Andy thought as he searched through the clutter of papers and model parts on his desk. Where is the other decal for this airplane? I bet Michelle was in here messing with my things again.

He knew his little sister didn't care about model airplanes, but she did like stickers. And decals probably looked like stickers to a five-year-old. He sighed. Sisters!

"Andy!" His mother's voice sounded muffled through the closed door of his bedroom. "Andy, would you come down here, please? Dad and I want to talk to you."

Muffled or not, something about her voice gave Andy a prickly feeling at the back of his neck. Had he done something wrong? He couldn't remember breaking anything. He hadn't lost any of his school books yet and it was October already. And he hadn't teased Michelle about her freckles for a long time. Anyway, she was spending the afternoon at a friend's house.

Mom and Dad had been arguing a lot, but the counseling sessions they'd been going to seemed to help. Anyway, why would Mom call him to come downstairs if the two of them weren't getting along again?

"C'mon, Jake," he said. His new puppy jumped off the bed and looked up at him, wagging his tail.

Andy opened the door and started downstairs, taking his almost-finished model with him. Jake thumped down the steps behind him, nearly stepping on his own ears.

His parents were standing a few feet apart in the living room, waiting for him. Mom kept rubbing her hands together as if she were washing them. Dad was tapping his foot, like he always did when he was nervous. The prickly feeling came back.

"Andy, Mom and I have something to tell you," his father began. Then he stopped and cleared his throat. "Son, you know your mother and I are trying to work things out between us, going to counseling and all. We've . . . we've finally decided we need to spend a couple of months apart and think things over."

Andy used his thumbnail to scrape a glob of glue off the wing of his airplane. Airplanes should look neat, he told himself, just like the picture on the box.

"This isn't a divorce, Andy." Mom said quietly. "It's just a time for us to sort things out."

Dad nodded. "I'm going to stay in an apartment in Springfield, near my company's main office."

Maybe I should look on the floor under my desk, Andy thought. I bet that's where my decal is.

"Springfield is only about an hour and a half from here," his mother said. "You'll be able to stay with Dad on weekends, if you want. Michelle can go with you sometimes, too." Her voice sounded funny again, kind of stiff.

Andy noticed the flap on one wing didn't move up and down like it was supposed to. Glue must have got in the wrong place, he thought. He tried to jiggle it loose, but it broke off in his hand.

"Andy? Did you hear what Dad said?" His mom lifted his chin with her hand and tried to make him look at her.

He pulled away. "Yeah. Okay. Can I go back upstairs now?" Couldn't they see he was trying to finish his model? Now he had to fix the darned flap, too. "C'mon, Jake."

"Andy, wait . . . ," his mother called as he ran up the steps.

"Just give him some time, Carol," he heard his father say.

Andy closed the door tightly as soon as he got in his room. He searched the floor under his desk for the decal, but all he found was gum wrappers. An hour later he was still trying to glue the flap back on when his dad called him to come downstairs again.

As soon as Andy started down the steps, he saw the suitcases, three of them. They formed a low wall between his mom and dad.

His mother was staring at the floor. Dad was carrying Michelle, who hugged his neck as if she'd never let go. Andy wished she'd stop crying so he could ask her about his decal.

"Andy, I'm leaving now, but I'll call you as soon as I get to Springfield. Do you want to come and stay with me this weekend?"

Andy thought it over and shook his head. "Pete and I are going to a movie."

His father handed Michelle to her mother and walked over to Andy. He put his hands on his son's shoulders. "I'm going to miss you, Tiger." He sounded as if he had a cold.

"I've got to take Jake for a walk." Andy pushed past his dad and held the door open for his dog. As he hurried out after him, he heard Dad tell Mom, "It's okay. Let him go for now."

His father had left by the time Andy and Jake got back, but his mom was waiting for him.

"Want to go out with Michelle and me for hamburgers and fries?" Her smile didn't hide her red-rimmed eyes.

"Nah. I'm not hungry." He headed back upstairs to look for his decal. Maybe it had fallen in his waste basket.

"We'll bring you back a hamburger anyway," Mom called up the steps. "Maybe you'll be hungry later, honey. And maybe we could sit and talk for a while."

But when he heard them come back home a little later, Andy lay down on his bed. He pretended to be asleep when his mom peeked in the room. The last thing he needed was a little talk. What did they have to talk about, anyway? Mom ought to be talking to Dad, not to him!

Andy never did find the decal, but everything was pretty normal the rest of the week. Except for Michelle. She was being a real baby.

"Is Daddy coming home tonight?" she asked again at dinner on Thursday.

"Michelle!" he yelled. "You asked that about six thousand times so far. Stop it!"

"Andy! She's upset! It's okay!" His mom reached over and hugged Michelle. "This is a hard time for all of us."

"Not me," he mumbled. But now he wasn't hungry.

On Saturday afternoon, Pete rang the doorbell and then barged right into the house.

"You don't live here, you know!" Andy growled at him.

"But I always do that!"

"Well, it's rude and crude."

Pete just looked at him for a minute. "Are you ready to go to the movies? My dad can take us." Then Pete bit his lip. "I mean . . . maybe my mom will drive."

"Hey, I know you still have a father. I do, too. He just doesn't live here right now. It's no big thing."

Pete nodded quickly. "Right. Well, are you ready to go?"

Andy rubbed his forehead. "I have a headache. I'm going upstairs where it's quiet." He headed for the steps.

"What about the movies?" Pete asked.

"Not today," Andy muttered. Pete just didn't know when to quit.

"Well, do you want to work on models then?" Pete asked. "I got a new one. I'll go get it!"

"Maybe tomorrow," Andy mumbled as he reached the top step. He went into his room and slammed the door, but that made his head feel worse. A real friend wouldn't keep bugging me, he told himself.

The next morning Andy was sitting with his mom in the kitchen, staring at a bowl of soggy cereal, when Michelle came downstairs.

"What's wrong with you?" he asked.

Her face was red and blotchy, as if she'd been crying, but she was smiling. "Jake slept in my bed last night, not yours!"

"The dog slept with you last night?" her mom asked with a worried frown. She tilted Michelle's face up to the light.

"What's wrong with her anyway?" Andy demanded.

His mother's shoulders seemed to droop. "She must be allergic to Jake." She closed her eyes and shook her head.

"Well, so what? Stay away from my dog, Michelle!"

"She can't do that in this small house, Andy. Anyway, Jake was supposed to be her dog, too."

His mom didn't say any more, but Andy decided to shut Jake in his bedroom every night. That would keep him from sleeping with Michelle again. Tuesday evening, though, his sister sat on the kitchen floor to color. Jake kept climbing in her lap and licking her face. Soon her eyes were red again and her nose was running.

"C'mon, Jake," Andy called. "Let's go for a walk." He had to get the dog away from Michelle before his mom noticed what was happening. Sisters!

Things at school weren't much better. On Wednesday, a kid named Karl brushed by Andy's table in the cafeteria and knocked half his sandwich on the floor. Andy could tell Karl did it on purpose. He jumped up and grabbed Karl's shirt just as the principal walked into the cafeteria.

The principal took him to her office and called his mother, just as he expected. But when he got home after school, his mom wasn't mad.

She even hugged him. "Andy, you've never been in trouble at school before. This is just a hard time. . . ."

"Not for me! Why can't you believe that!" He tried to pull away, but she held him tightly.

"Oh, Andy, I know you must feel angry right now, but you can't handle it by beating up kids at school. Can't we talk about it? You'll feel a lot better. . . ."

"Mom, I can handle this! I am handling it! Anyway, it's time for Jake's walk." At least his dog didn't want to talk all the time.

But Saturday afternoon, things did get bad. His father showed up to take Jake to live with him in Springfield.

"Jake can't stay here, Andy," his mother said. "Michelle's allergies are getting worse. Her eyes start to water when the dog comes near her."

"This way, you can still see Jake when you come and stay with me," his dad explained. "We're lucky I'm allowed to keep a dog in my apartment."

Lucky! They didn't understand at all! "You can't take Jake!" Tears rushed to his eyes, surprising Andy more than anyone. "You can't take away my dog!"

> "Everyone cries sometimes, Andy. Even grown-ups. And everyone feels sad sometimes, especially times like this."

"Andy, let's go out in the backyard for a while, okay?" His dad was already pulling him toward the back door. He didn't have a choice.

As soon as his father opened the door, Jake rushed out into the small yard, yipping happily. Dad led Andy over to the old wooden park bench under their only tree. His father settled back on the bench, but Andy sat on the edge of his seat. He had sniffed back his tears, but he couldn't get rid of the lump in his throat.

"I know you'll miss Jake," his father said, "but I'll take good care of him. You can come and see him a lot, maybe every weekend if we can arrange it."

His dad pulled him close. "I really miss you, Andy. I miss all of you." His words seemed to catch in his throat. "I'm feeling pretty sad and lonely right now."

Andy kept his body stiff. "If you take Jake away, I don't know what I'll do." His eyes were burning.

"Don't you miss *me* a little, Andy?"

Suddenly Andy's face crumpled. He put his arms around his dad's neck and cried for the first time in at least a year. Finally he pulled back and looked at his dad. His father's eyes were a little shiny, too.

"I guess Michelle's not the only baby in this family. I'm not as grown up as I thought," Andy admitted in a hoarse voice.

His dad smiled and brushed back Andy's hair. "Everyone cries sometimes, Andy. Even grown-ups. And everyone feels sad sometimes, especially times like this."

"I really do miss you, Dad." The tears started again, but this time Andy let them fall.

After a few minutes, Andy took a big breath and looked up at his dad again. "Are you busy next weekend? Could I come and play with Jake and see where you live?"

"Why don't you come back with me today? You can help me get Jake settled. He might feel better if you're there the first night in his new home. I'll bring you back here tomorrow night."

• •

Andy nodded. His heart felt a little lighter. He watched Jake try to catch a bird flying overhead. "I'll explain it all to Jake on the way to Springfield. I'll tell him it's okay if he feels sad at first. And I'll tell him I'll always love him, even if I don't see him every day."

FACTUAL QUESTIONS:

1. What is the situation Andy faces?

_____

2. When he learns about the situation, how does he react?

_____

3. How does Andy respond when his sister shows her emotions?

_____

4. What are some ways Andy's parents encourage him to share his feelings? How does he react?

_____

_____

5. What finally causes Andy to accept and share what he is feeling?

_____

INTERPRETIVE QUESTIONS:

6. What are some emotions Andy probably experiences as the reality of the situation sinks in? What emotions or attitudes does he communicate?

_____

_____

7. Why do you think Andy seems so concerned about working on his model?

_____

_____

8. What are some ways Andy's true feelings about the situation begin to affect his behavior?

_____

_____

9. Why do you think the loss of his dog bothers Andy so much?

_____

_____

10. How do you think Andy's behavior will change after the conversation with his father at the end of the story?

_____

_____

11. What are some more positive ways Andy could have dealt with his emotions? What are some ways he could have communicated to his family how he was feeling?

_____

_____

LOOKING BACK

NAME: _____ DATE: _____

• •

Look back at the reasons you wrote at the beginning of this unit. In the spaces below, copy your two reasons why feelings can lead to problems sometimes. Then, using what you've learned in this unit, describe ways you can handle the feeling and the situation so it isn't so likely to lead to problems.

REASON #1: _____

_____

Ways I can handle the situation better: _____

_____

_____

_____

_____

REASON #2: _____

_____

Ways I can handle the situation better: _____

_____

_____

_____

_____

TIP: *When you understand and express your feelings, you'll have control over them. They won't control you.*

UNIT 4
IMPROVING PEER
RELATIONSHIPS

Friendship is very important to you. You may be asking yourself, "Do I have any real friends? Can I trust my friends with my secrets? Will they still want me for a friend if I do something stupid or different from what they do? Will they try to make me do things I don't really want to do? Would they like me if they knew the *real* me?"

Most people your age ask themselves these same questions. Here are some comments from a few of them:

I love being around my friends. They're nice, considerate, and caring. I feel safe and happy with them, and I know I'm not alone.

What bothers me most is the way some kids act fake in front of people, or they think they're too cool to talk to others. I try to be nice to everyone and help anyone who needs it.

Honesty is a big part of being a friend. If you can't tell the truth or if you're always talking about people behind their backs, who needs you as a friend? You have to be kind to others to have people be kind back to you. You have to be a friend to have a friend.

Friends are people you can be weak with. They let you be yourself. They let you make mistakes and be a fool. They forgive you. They're always there when you need them.

I never expected to get into an argument with my best friend that lasted for more than a week, but it happened recently. We've been friends for ten years.

It's difficult to have more than one best friend because the other one gets jealous.

My friend and I went to our old school, sat on the monkey bars, and talked for two hours. It felt great!

This unit is about friendship. It will help you recognize the qualities of a true friend and look at some ways you can reach out and make new friends. In the discussions and activities you'll take a hard look at peer pressure. You'll learn what you can do and say to stand up for your own beliefs and values and still keep friendships.

Friendship is like a seed—it grows when it receives love and attention. Decide to be the kind of friend you'd like to have yourself.

Barbara Varenhorst is the author of the article in this unit, "Deciding to Be the Friend You Want." She has written a whole book for teenagers about friendship. She's also the founder of a program that teaches students how to be peer counselors. She understands how difficult it can be sometimes to make the right choices when peer pressure is involved.

The short story for this unit, "Between Friends," focuses on changes in friendships. It tells about two 13-year-olds who are going off on different life paths. Through the story we see that "growing apart" can be a sad time in a friendship—but it's also part of growing up.

GETTING STARTED

Read the quotes again. You probably have some definite opinions about friendship—and some questions. In the space below, write two questions you have about friendship.

Question 1:_____

_____

_____

_____

Question 2:_____

_____

_____

_____

Look for answers to your questions as you participate in the discussions and activities in this unit.

UNIT 4
UNIT PROJECTS

• •

Complete at least one unit project by working on your own, with a partner, or with the class.

1. Set a goal to meet one or two new people every week during this unit. Make it a point to meet people of various ages and ethnic groups and use your communication skills to get to know these people. Describe your experience in a report or in some other creative way. Possible topics to include:

   • A brief description of each person you met.
   • How you met.
   • Things you talked about.
   • What you like about that person.
   • Something you learned as a result of meeting that person.

2. Set up committees and plan a Friendship Festival at school. Include movies, speakers, workshops, resources, and activities to make people more aware of friendship issues and skills. Consider these ideas:

   • Write compliments on slips of paper and present them to each student.
   • Place posters with messages about friendship around the school.
   • Invite students from different cultures or ethnic groups to share traditional ways of expressing friendship.
   • Write poetry or songs about friendship.

3. Work with several classmates to write a play about friendship. Rehearse until you can do it well and then present it to the class.

4. Organize a friendship panel discussion, including panelists who represent different age groups, ethnic backgrounds, and points of view. These might include elementary, junior high or middle, and high school students, parents, and elderly people. Prepare questions about friendship for the panelists to discuss.

LOOKING AT FRIENDSHIP

NAME: _____ DATE: _____

• •

Write as many responses as you can think of in each category below.

POSITIVE FRIENDSHIP	NEGATIVE FRIENDSHIP

POSITIVE FRIENDSHIP

Some reasons for a positive friendship:

_____

_____

_____

_____

_____

Things positive friends might do together:

_____

_____

_____

_____

_____

NEGATIVE FRIENDSHIP

Some reasons for a negative friendship:

_____

_____

_____

_____

Things negative friends might do together:

_____

_____

_____

A way out of a negative friendship:

_____

_____

_____

TIP: *A real friend doesn't say "I'll be your friend if. . . ." Real friends won't push you to do something you know is wrong for you.*

99

INSIDE PRESSURE SITUATIONS

NAME: _____ DATE: _____

Describe two situations in which inside pressure might lead people your age to do something negative or harmful. Write the negative message and the positive message to counteract it.

SITUATION 1:	SITUATION 2:
_____	_____
_____	_____
_____	_____
A **negative** message that a person in this situation might be thinking:	A **negative** message that a person in this situation might be thinking:
_____	_____
_____	_____
_____	_____
A **positive** inside message that could contradict the negative thinking:	A **positive** inside message that could contradict the negative thinking:
_____	_____
_____	_____
_____	_____
_____	_____

ASK Information Sheet

NAME: _____ DATE: _____

Sometimes we get into trouble because we don't ask enough
questions. When someone encourages you to do something you
think might lead to trouble, use the three steps of ASK.

A — ASK QUESTIONS

Ask questions so you know what you're getting into. Then you can
decide if the situation could lead to trouble. Here are some things
you need to know—or find out by asking questions:

• Is it against the law, rules, or the teachings of my religion?

• Is it harmful to me or to others?

• Would it disappoint my family or other important adults?

• Is it wrong to do? (Would I be sorry afterward?)

• Would I be hurt or upset if someone did this to me?

S — SAY NO TO NEGATIVE PRESSURE

If the answer to any of the questions above is
"Yes," your response to the pressure to join in
should be "No."

K — KNOW POSITIVE OPTIONS

Know some positive activities and suggest one of
them. If the person insists on the negative
activity, leave. The person might decide to join
you later.

PRACTICING ASK

NAME: _____ DATE: _____

On a separate sheet of paper, describe a situation that involves negative peer pressure. Pretend Chris and Pat are in this situation. Describe how Chris might ask Pat to join in an activity, without making it clear what Chris actually has in mind. What might Chris say?

A — ASK QUESTIONS

What are two or three questions Pat could ask to find out what Chris actually wants to do?

_____

_____

_____

How might Chris answer these questions?

_____

_____

_____

Do you think this situation will lead to trouble? _____

S — SAY NO TO NEGATIVE PRESSURE

If the situation could lead to trouble, what could Pat say?

_____

_____

K — KNOW POSITIVE OPTIONS

What positive activities could Pat suggest?

_____

_____

What should Pat do if Chris rejects his suggestions?

_____

_____

ASSERTIVE RESISTANCE
SITUATIONS

NAME: _____ DATE: _____

Choose a situation and show your group members how you would resist it assertively.

1. Some friends want you to sneak out Friday night after the curfew you and your parents have agreed on. You don't want to betray your parents' trust.

2. Your friends are really angry at a person who they say started some rumors. You're sure this person is innocent.

3. Several friends want you to help them throw eggs at someone's home. You know that's vandalism and you don't want to participate.

4. Your friends want you to wear clothes or a hairstyle that makes you feel uncomfortable.

5. Several friends want to shoplift while you're with them. You know shoplifting is wrong.

6. A friend has a copy of tomorrow's math test. This person invites you over to look at it. You know that's cheating.

7. After you eat at the local pizza place, some friends want to distract the waitress and leave without paying. You know that's wrong and the waitress would have to pay for your pizza herself.

8. A friend wants you to tell his parents he was at your house last night, even though he wasn't. You know lying is wrong.

9. When you and a friend are walking home from school, you see someone drop a $5 bill. Your friend picks it up and wants to keep it. You want to give it back.

10. Some friends want you to ask your parents for a stereo. You know your family can't afford it.

Let people know what you stand for—and what you won't stand for.
—H. Jackson Brown, Jr.

DECIDING TO BE THE FRIEND YOU WANT

BY BARBARA VARENHORST

Many of us work hard to change our outer selves so we'll get the right label—"cool," "popular," or whatever.

What are you going to be when you grow up, Charlie Brown?

Lonesome.

Charlie's answer may make you laugh—a little. But now that you're growing up yourself, you may not think it's so funny. You're in early adolescence; things inside and outside you have changed and are still changing. Maybe you feel lonesome at times—or afraid and confused. Maybe you're concerned about having friends and being popular.

The confusion and loneliness are real. Sometimes other people may brush off your feelings and tell you not to worry. Not being understood just adds to the loneliness.

This is normal. Every one of your classmates has similar feelings and thoughts, even though it may not seem that way. Friends can be really helpful at these times. That's why everyone your age needs help to learn how to become the kind of friend others want and need.

THE CHOICES YOU'LL HAVE TO MAKE

The decisions young people face in friendships fall into three large "baskets." Each basket contains major choices that affect who you are, the kinds of friends you will have, and what you will do with your life. One basket is labeled *Peer Pressure Decisions;* another, *Hide or Reveal Yourself Decisions;* and the third, *Giving and Receiving Decisions.* I'm going to describe each basket and suggest ways to handle each kind of decision.

PEER PRESSURE DECISIONS

Before you can deal effectively with peer pressure decisions, you need to think about who you really are and what you really want. Sometimes that isn't so easy. Each of us carries around two selves. One is our outer self—how we look, what we wear, and what we say or do. The other self is the inner self that few people know or see.

Because we want people to like and admire us, many of us work hard to change our outer selves so we'll get the right label—"cool," "popular," or whatever. We try to say the right things, wear the right clothes, and even pretend to know things to impress others. Some people call this playing a role or being phony.

The inner person that people can't see is who you *really* are. This self doesn't change every time you change your appearance. The more you are true to your inner self, the more alike your inner and outer selves will be.

WHO DECIDES FOR YOU? YOU OR YOUR FRIENDS?

Most people your age have a great fear of being mocked—of being considered weird or different. What if your classmates laugh, put you down, or shut you out of the group? Some people might be willing to do anything to keep that from happening. When their fear is this great, they may be so eager to be liked that they're willing to let their peers decide things for them. That is called "peer pressure."

Negative peer pressure is a problem because it encourages us to adopt negative attitudes and participate in negative activities. Positive peer pressure, encouraging friends to do positive things, can help others make the most of their lives.

Peer pressure can be a powerful influence, so let's examine how it works. If we understand the different ways it affects us, we may be better able to resist it when it leads to harmful attitudes and activities.

Suppose the most popular boy in the class asks to borrow your notes to study for an important test tomorrow. You'd planned on using the notes yourself. What will you do? What if your best friend wants you to skip school? Would you do it to keep the friendship? What if everyone else is making fun of someone? Do you think the other kids would like you more if you joined in?

Suppose your parents have forbidden you to go to a certain movie. Some of your friends are going to see it this Saturday afternoon. You tell them you can't go, but they say you'll miss the best movie of the year. So you decide "just this once" to lie to your parents and tell them you have a baby-sitting job. And suppose that while you're at the movie, the mother you said you were baby-sitting for calls your home and wants to talk to you. Your lie is discovered. Besides being punished, you've lost your parents' trust. Now they may question your honesty in all situations. That's quite a high price to pay for a movie.

At such times it may help to ask yourself why your "friends" would try to get you to do something you don't want to do or know you shouldn't do. Why would friends try to get you to lie to your parents, be unkind to others, or even try drugs? It's possible they're trying to make themselves feel more grown-up or cool. They will look more important if you and others go along with them. It's also possible they're not really your friends.

One of the basic laws of human life is that things are to be used and people are to be loved. When others want you to do something harmful or wrong to serve their own needs, they are using you. But people can't use you unless you let them. Are you going to let others use you, or are you going to decide for yourself?

SOME TIPS ON HOW TO DECIDE FOR YOURSELF

By giving in to peer pressure, you may actually lose the respect of those you hope to impress. No one really values someone who can be used, manipulated, or pressured. For a while those who pressure you may fake friendship, but they may ignore you when you are no longer useful to them.

But what if you told your friends, "I can't go with you to the movie on Saturday. My parents said I can't, and I don't want to go against their wishes." Even if you think your parents are being too strict, you'll like yourself a lot more if you follow their rules than if you lie to them.

It takes strength to refuse to go along with the crowd. Consider how much strength it must have taken in the following true story. It took place in a fairly typical high school where most of the students spend a lot of their time worrying about what others think. In this high school, if you are anybody, you belong to a clique, and the clique decides how you dress and what you do and say.

Each morning before class, all the cliques gather around the school's courtyard to watch each other and check out what is going on. No one walks across the courtyard because they might get laughed at.

One rainy morning, a girl carrying a load of books started across the courtyard. She must have been a new student because she didn't know the rules. In the middle of the courtyard, she tripped and fell, spread-eagled, her books all over. Immediately the jeering and laughter erupted. Then a boy walked toward her. As he got nearer, the laughter began to fade. He helped her up and picked up her books. As the two of them walked away, there was utter silence. Then, still in silence, the cliques began to drift away.

This boy had the courage to stand up to powerful peer pressure. What would you have done if you had been in the crowd that morning? What would your friends have done?

CAN YOU LEARN TO SAY "NO"?

Most of the decisions you'll make won't be as dramatic as that. But they will come up suddenly, when you least expect them, giving you little time to think. People who want to make their own decisions and not be pressured by their peers are prepared with a plan for handling such situations.

A simple, honest, "No, I don't want to" or "Sorry, I can't" can be an effective way of handling negative peer pressure. If you practice saying these phrases alone at home, you will gain courage to say them to others when you need to.

You can say "No" to peer pressure without coming across as rude, aggressive, or self-righteous. The best approach is to be assertive—calm and confident of your decision to resist negative pressure. Remember that you have a right to say "No" and to expect others to accept your decision.

WILL YOU LOSE YOUR FRIENDS?

Sometimes friendships have to be tested. A real friend doesn't say "I'll be your friend if. . . ." A real friend says "I'll be your friend and support you."

If you frequently disagree with what your friends want to do, maybe you need to find new friends who support you and your values.

HIDE OR REVEAL YOURSELF DECISIONS

You're at an age when having friends seems to be one of the most important things in life. It may be tempting to go along with the crowd in order to keep them as friends. But real friendship is almost the opposite of going along with negative peer pressure.

Why is this so? One of the main consequences of giving in to peer pressure is that you may be faking who you are, and your friendships will also be fake. Real friends can say to each other, "Here I am. Take me or leave me." To say that, and to live it, takes courage.

Some young people are so fearful of revealing their true selves that they build shells around themselves for protection. The shell keeps others away and makes them feel safe from criticism or ridicule. Many people who act stuck-up or egotistical are really fearful of revealing themselves. People who appear gruff or unkind may actually be tenderhearted under their shells.

Why do you suppose people put on these shells? Author John Powell offers an answer: "I'm afraid to tell you who I am, because if I tell you who I am, you may not like who I am, and it's all that I have."

HOW WILL YOU SHARE YOURSELF WITH OTHERS?

Whether to hide or reveal yourself is an important decision. Revealing yourself is often the first step toward making real friends. Let me explain what I mean by revealing yourself.

If you were to list the qualities of a friend, you would probably include that a friend is someone you can trust and talk with openly. That means a person who is willing to share personal feelings.

We all have some feelings we talk about with almost anyone—such as how we feel about a teacher, a movie, or a popular song.

We also have some feelings we don't talk about very often—such as fears, shame or disappointment, or even pride or joy. And we tend to hide feelings that confuse or bother us.

The best approach is to be assertive—calm and confident of your decision to resist negative pressure.

Being open about feelings makes the difference between just knowing someone and being friends. The feelings you don't talk about are often the core of who you are. If you don't share them, no one will ever know who you really are!

Of course, other things draw friends together besides sharing feelings. Having the same interests and learning skills or hobbies from one another are an important part of friendship. A friend is someone with whom you share fun adventures, long conversations, and just being together.

GIVING AND RECEIVING DECISIONS

We all need friends, but not just to satisfy our own needs or make us feel less lonely. Wanting friends for these reasons isn't bad. But if these are our only reasons for wanting friends, we're using people. Real friendship means giving, caring, and doing for others. One way people make friends is by giving friendship without expecting anything in return.

I know this is true after helping hundreds of young people become involved with others through the peer counseling program that I direct. Through this program, we learn how to help and support each other through practicing effective listening skills and demonstrating that we care about each other. I have seen many students join with others to turn peer pressure into peer support. Here's one true and vivid example:

People your age can be extremely sensitive to the needs of others. They can learn to reach out. You can do this, too.

Gloria's personality was not very appealing. Early in peer counseling training, she began to talk about her many problems. She had few friends, her home situation was miserable, and she didn't like herself. Even though she was seeing a counselor regularly, she couldn't shake her sad feelings. I became deeply concerned but kept this concern to myself.

As the sessions progressed, I began to sense a difference in Gloria. Something was happening. Then, during our last session, I found out why. The other students in the group had also sensed Gloria's needs. Without my knowledge, they had organized themselves to make daily contact with her, even on the weekends. They would check in with her to see how she was doing or just stop to have a friendly chat. Now, as the class was ending, Gloria told the group what this had meant. She said she couldn't have made it without their friendship. She now felt there was a reason for living.

These 13-year-olds proved that people your age can be extremely sensitive to the needs of others. They can learn to reach out. You can do this, too. You don't need a peer counseling class to get started. You do need the desire.

HOW CAN YOU BE A GOOD FRIEND?

What are *you* going to be when you grow up?

"A caring friend who likes myself, who makes decisions for myself based on my values, and who is willing to share my feelings with others." Is this your reply? I hope so.

. . . .

In the African country of Ghana stands a large statue of a hand holding an egg. The message is that if the hand holds the egg too loosely, it will fall out and break. But if the hand holds it too firmly, the egg will be crushed.

We can learn something about friendship from this statue. It takes a certain kind of person to reach out to others and to protect and support the friendships that develop. Decide what kind of friend you would like to support you. Then become that kind of person yourself.

FACTUAL QUESTIONS:

1. What are the three "baskets" of decisions about friendships? Why does Barbara Varenhorst say they're important?

_____

_____

2. How does the author define *peer pressure?* When does she believe peer pressure becomes a problem?

_____

_____

3. Describe one way the author says someone could give in to peer pressure and lose his or her parents' trust.

_____

_____

4. How can we learn to say "No" to negative peer pressure?

_____

_____

5. What does the author think you should do if you're frequently in conflict with your friends?

_____

_____

6. What does the author mean by "revealing yourself" in a friendship?

_____

_____

7. What do we need to give to others in order to make friends?

_____

_____

· ·

INTERPRETIVE QUESTIONS:

8. Why do you think peers sometimes pressure others to do things that can lead to trouble?

_____

_____

9. What are the benefits of making decisions based on your own best judgment rather than on pressure from peers?

_____

_____

10. Why do you think Barbara Varenhorst believes that "real friendship is almost the opposite of going along with peer pressure"?

_____

_____

11. The author writes that things are to be used and people are to be loved. What does she mean?

_____

_____

12. Why is Gloria's story important?

_____

_____

Friends are like walls. Sometimes you lean on them, and sometimes it's enough just to know they're there.

SOLVED

NAME: _____ DATE: _____

Complete this worksheet with your partner.

State the problem as you see it.

Person 1: _____

_____

Open the discussion to other points of view

Person 2: _____

_____

List the possible solutions together.

(Illegal or harmful solutions are not considered.)

_____

_____

_____

_____

Veto the solutions that are unacceptable to someone involved.

(Cross out any unacceptable solutions in the step above.)

Evaluate the positive solutions that are left.

What are the advantages and disadvantages of each one?

Do the one most acceptable to everyone.

How well did the solution work? (Or: How will you know how well the solution worked?)

_____

_____

TIP: *The best way to get rid of a problem is to solve it.*

111

BETWEEN FRIENDS

Wilson was in his room doing his homework when the phone rang. He heard his mother answer it in the kitchen. Then her voice came echoing up the stairs: "Wilson! For you. Don't stay on long—I'm expecting some calls from my church group."

Wilson padded out to the hall in his stocking feet, plopped down on the carpet, and picked up the phone that lay on the floor.

"Gotta go, Nathan," Wilson said. But he wished Nathan would say something—anything.

"Who were the Bulls playing when Michael Jordan scored 63 points in one game?" It was Nathan.

Wilson thought for a moment. "Uhh . . . Let's see . . . The Cavaliers?"

"No! The Celtics. I'm so disappointed in you."

"Yeah, well, I guess I must be losing my touch. Anyway, I can't talk now, okay? My mom's expecting some calls."

"Okay, I'll see ya 'round school tomorrow."

"I won't be in school tomorrow—remember?"

"You playing hooky or something?" Nathan asked.

"I already told you! Tomorrow is the day I take the test to get into Richmond High. Now I gotta go so I can rest my mind after all this heavy thinking."

On the other end of the line was a long silence. To Wilson, the silence was loud.

"Wilson!" His mother called from the kitchen. "Are you still on?"

"Gotta go, Nathan," Wilson said. But he wished Nathan would say something—anything.

Finally Nathan spoke. "Don't think too hard, Mr. Genius. It might burn out your brain." The phone clicked as he hung up.

Wilson hung up too. Then he called downstairs, "I'm off, Mom. Sorry."

"I just wish I didn't have to keep asking you." His mother came to the bottom of the steps.

"But Mom," Wilson said in a playful tone, "I'm a teenager. I'm supposed to be difficult."

"Very funny."

"Anyway," he told her, "you don't need to worry about me and Nathan spending so much time on the phone any more. If I get in to Richmond High, he'll probably never talk to me again."

"That is *not* very funny," Wilson's mother said. "If it were true, I'd be very, very sorry."

Just then the phone rang. "That's for me, I'm sure." She rushed back to the kitchen.

Wilson was glad for the interruption. If they had kept talking, he might have admitted how upset he was. For weeks now, he and Nathan had been arguing about Wilson taking the test for Richmond High. Richmond was a magnet school with lots of science and math courses. The kids with the best grades went there, the ones who wanted to be doctors and biologists and engineers.

For Nathan, school was a kind of game; his object was to avoid as much work as possible, unless it was learning basketball trivia. Wilson had a completely different attitude about school, but he'd almost rather not go to Richmond High than lose his best and oldest friend.

The day after the test, Wilson was walking down the hall of Franklin Junior High toward his English honors class. He was still thinking about the test and didn't notice Nathan coming toward him.

"Hey, man! What's up?" Nathan asked.

Wilson smiled as he stuck out his hand for their usual handshake. "Hey!"

Wilson noticed a strange glint in Nathan's eye as Nathan squeezed Wilson's hand extra hard.

"How many times was Kareem voted most valuable player?" Nathan asked.

"That's easy! Six. Give me something more challenging."

"Why? So you can exercise your brain some more?" Nathan asked.

"Come on, Nathan. Don't start bugging me about that. Just give me another question."

"Okay. I got a good one. Who was the tallest player in NBA history?"

"Hmm. I gotta think about that one."

"Come on, Mr. Brain. You should know this! Haven't you been reading that sports trivia book I gave you for your birthday?"

"Give me a break! I've been sort of busy. Wait! I think I know! Manuel Bol?"

"*Manute* Bol!"

"Hey, I was close. Now I gotta run. I gotta get to English class," Wilson said.

The look in Nathan's eyes was downright unfriendly. "Oh, you wouldn't dream of being late. You wouldn't dream of making dear Mrs. Benson mad."

Suddenly Wilson was angry, too. "Lay off it, Nathan. I gotta go."

"Yeah," Nathan said. "You gotta go to fancy English honors class, and you gotta go to fancy Richmond High School, too."

So that was it! "All I did was take the test," Wilson said. "I didn't say I was gonna go. I may not even get in."

"Oh, you'll get in," Nathan said. "And then you'll go. And then you'll turn into this creepy kid I won't even recognize. I bet the only thing the kids at Richmond High think about is what universities they're applying to."

The bell rang. "Now I *am* late," Wilson said. "Thanks a lot. Thanks for nothing. Some friend you are."

Wilson spent the rest of the day thinking about what Nathan had said. By the time dinner rolled around, he was pretty depressed. He was just glad that dinner at the Davis house usually meant everyone trying to talk at once: Wilson, his older brother and sister, and their parents. Tonight he hoped his usual part in the conversation wouldn't be missed.

He made it through dinner okay. Then there was a break in the chatter as everybody paid some serious attention to a chocolate pie 16-year-old Aisha had made.

"Wilson," said his father, "you're awfully quiet tonight. I have a feeling something's bothering you. Got a problem?"

"I'd rather not talk about it," Wilson said. The rest of the family stared at him. "It's something . . . I don't want to talk about it."

"I bet I know," said Arthur, Wilson's brother. "It's about Nathan." Arthur played basketball with Wilson and Nathan sometimes.

Wilson clenched his teeth. "I don't want to talk about it."

Wilson's father looked at him a minute. Then he said, "Arthur and Aisha, please clean up tonight. Wilson, I think you and your mom and I need to talk."

When the three of them were seated in comfortable chairs in the living room, Wilson's father said, "We have to know what's bothering you, son. This is not a family where people keep secrets from each other."

> *"I don't think there's much you can do."* Wilson stared at the floor.

"Just tell us about it," his mother said quietly. "Sometimes when you just talk, things don't seem so bad."

"I've been thinking . . .," Wilson began. His parents waited patiently. "I've been thinking that even if I get in to Richmond High, I'm not going there. I can go to Jones High, where all the other kids are going. Where Nathan's going."

Wilson's father looked at his wife. Then he turned to Wilson and asked, "Is that what you really want to do?"

"I don't know."

"You don't know, Wilson?" his mother said. "After all your hard work at school, you don't know what your goal is? Tell me, who was saying the other day he wanted to go to a good university and become a doctor so he could help other people? Was that you? Or was that someone else?"

For a minute, Wilson didn't say anything. Tears stung his eyes. "I don't want to lose my friends!"

"Yes," his father said. "Your friends are very important. Friends *should* be important. But tell me, son, what direction is Nathan going? What is his goal? Is it the same as yours?"

"I don't know what *my* goal is any more!" Wilson said.

"Well," his mother said, "goals don't mean anything unless you really believe in them."

Wilson's father nodded. "If you go to Richmond High School, it won't be for our benefit. If you decide to do all that hard work, you'd better be darn sure you're doing it for yourself."

"So," his mother said, "it looks like you have some big decisions to make. Whatever you do, we believe it'll be what's right. We have a lot of confidence in you, Wilson."

"You mean it's up to me?" Wilson asked.

"We hope you'll go to Richmond High," his father said. "But it has to be something you really want. Otherwise, you're just going through the motions."

"I agree," his mother said. "I agree completely."

Wilson was more confused than ever. He'd expected them to be upset by the idea that he might not go to Richmond High, but here they were, being understanding. "I have homework to do," he said finally. "Excuse me."

Wilson lay on his bed for hours that night, listening to his radio and thinking. Every once in a while, he glanced over at an old photograph pinned to his bulletin board. It showed him and Nathan, arms around each other's shoulders, grinning for the camera. It had been taken four years earlier, the first summer they went to camp.

Finally Wilson got up, went out to the hallway, and dialed the number he'd dialed so many times before. Nathan answered the phone after half a ring.

"How many points did Wilt Chamberlain score when he set an NBA record in '62?" Wilson asked.

"In the whole season, or one game?"

"One game."

"Let's see. I think it was. . . 100?"

"Shoot! You weren't supposed to know that one."

"Hey! I got a brain, too, you know. I can even remember things. I'm smarter than you think," Nathan said.

"You're as smart as anyone I know."

"Well, thank you for the compliment," Nathan said mockingly. "What is this? You want to borrow money or something?"

Wilson took a deep breath. "I want you to know that I'm gonna go to Richmond High School—if I get in. And I think I *will* get in. I'm gonna go because I want to. It could be the most important thing I ever do in my life. I have to try."

Wilson waited for an answer. His heart was pounding fast.

"Yeah, I know," Nathan finally said. "It's okay."

"So lay off me, will ya? Stop talking about it the way you do. Okay? 'Cause I'm gonna do it no matter what you think."

Nathan sighed a long, loud sigh. "I hear ya. Sure. You gotta do what you gotta do."

"That's right. I gotta do *this.* For myself!"

"Look," Nathan said. "I better get some sleep. I'll catch ya later."

"Yeah. See ya." Slowly Wilson hung up the telephone.

For a long time he couldn't fall asleep. He just stared at the ceiling, trying not to look at the picture of himself and Nathan at camp. He wondered if their friendship would ever be the same. So much was changing.

One afternoon a few days later, Wilson was playing basketball in the schoolyard near his house. The basketball players were the usual crowd—Lonnie, James, Skip, Leroy, William, and some of the others. Wilson wondered where Nathan was, but he didn't ask.

Wilson wondered where Nathan was, but he didn't ask.

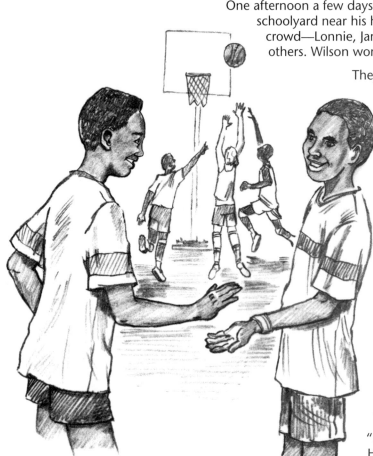

They hadn't talked since that night on the phone. Since most of Wilson's classes were honors sections, they could have gone for days without seeing each other at school.

Sweat dampened Wilson's T-shirt as he played. Running and dodging, shooting from all over the court, he was starting to feel great. After a beautiful jump shot, he was startled to hear a familiar voice saying, "Way to go! Lookin' good!"

Nathan was smiling at him from the sidelines. *Really* smiling. "Hey, Nathan!" Wilson shouted. "Wanna play?"

"Yeah, sure." As Nathan jogged onto the court, he slapped Wilson's hand, gave him a big smile, and said, "How you doing?"

"I'm all right. How you doing?"

"All right."

After the game, the two boys walked home together.

"Hey, Wilson. They got hoops at Richmond High?" Nathan asked.

• •

"Sure! There's a court right outside the school. Some guys were playing when I went for my test. Why?"

"Well, I was thinking. If you plan on going to that school, I'll probably have to at least check out the neighborhood. You know, make sure it's all right and everything. I wouldn't want my best friend hanging out in some dump!"

Wilson was stunned. Then he began to realize that this was the beginning of a new and different kind of friendship.

FACTUAL QUESTIONS:

1. How do you know Wilson and Nathan are good friends at the beginning of the story?

_____

_____

2. In what ways are Wilson and Nathan similar? Different?

_____

_____

3. Why does Wilson want to go to Richmond High School?

_____

_____

4. Why is Nathan so angry?

_____

_____

5. How do Wilson's parents help him handle his problem?

_____

_____

INTERPRETIVE QUESTIONS:

6. Why is the decision about school difficult for Wilson?

_____

_____

7. How has the friendship changed by the end of the story?

_____

_____

• •

8. How are the situations in the story realistic? In what ways do you think they are unrealistic?

_____

_____

_____

9. How do we decide between our goals and our friendships if we have to choose between the two? What things do we have to think about?

_____

_____

_____

_____

LOOKING BACK

NAME: _____   DATE: _____

• •

Look back at the two questions you wrote about friendship at the
beginning of this unit. Write them again in the spaces below, and
this time add the answers. Use what you've learned from the
activities and discussions during this unit. If you're still not sure of
the answers, talk the questions over—with a friend!

Question 1: _____

_____

_____

My answer: _____

_____

_____

_____

Question 2: _____

_____

_____

My answer: _____

_____

_____

_____

_____

_____

UNIT 5
STRENGTHENING FAMILY RELATIONSHIPS

Here are some comments about families we've gathered from other people your age:

I wouldn't trade my family for anyone else's in the world. They are special to me, and I'm proud to call them mine. I guess I'm most proud of the feeling of togetherness we share wherever we are.

I wish my family could do more things together. One or the other of us is always busy or not in the mood to join in.

I admire my family. It's not perfect, but it's really terrific. My parents are divorced, but we still have love. When all else fails, we always have that to fall back on. Our love keeps us together, and it always will.

I'm 14 and pretty mature for my age. But whenever I get into trouble, I get sent to my room. It's mainly a problem with my mom. I think she sends me to my room because she's afraid of all the things that could happen to me. I wish she knew that sending me to my room is not the answer.

This may sound weird, but I really like it when I'm alone with my mom, it's completely quiet, and we're in the kitchen. We have to be in the kitchen. I don't know why, but I feel so comfortable just sitting on the counter, late at night, rapping with my mom. You'd have to meet her to understand. She's the most honest, open, loving, sincere person I know. And even when I lose my temper, I know she'll always be there.

Could all these kids be talking about the same thing? Families today are changing. You may live in a traditional family with two parents, a single-parent family, or some other kind of family. You may live in one home during the week and another one on weekends. You may share your home with brothers and sisters, stepbrothers and stepsisters, uncles, aunts, grandparents, or others. Whether it's one person or 20, those who love and care for you are your family.

Sometimes living in close quarters can be difficult. Yet many people agree that a family is the most precious and supportive group we have. Whatever your family is like, you might be able to strengthen it. Could you be more supportive and kind? Could you listen better? Do you show appreciation for the things your family does for you? Do you help out? Do you give back as much as you take—or more?

In this unit, "Strengthening Family Relationships," you'll have a chance to share something about your family and learn a little about your classmates' families. The class will talk with older people and find out how families have changed over the years. You'll help think of ways to use the skills you're learning in this program at home and plan some fun things for your family to do together.

The article for this unit was written by Charlie W. Shedd, a counselor who has helped families with almost any problem you can think of. In "You and Your Family," he describes many issues facing families such as housework, use of the telephone, curfews, and lots of others. The article also offers some basic rules about how to get along with your family. Follow them, and see how well they can work for you.

The short story, "No Party for Nancy," contrasts two families. Nancy's parents want to know where she is and what she's doing. Claudia's parents let her do whatever she wants, and they hardly seem to care. Who do you think is better off? The story answers this question in a way that may surprise you.

By the time you finish this unit, you'll know just how special and important *your* family really is. By the way—don't forget to tell them!

GETTING STARTED

Read the quotes again. Think about reasons why young people have such different feelings about their families. Then list four things that might strengthen the relationships in a typical family.

Here's my list of ways to strengthen family relationships:

_____

_____

_____

_____

_____

UNIT 5
UNIT PROJECTS

Complete at least one unit project by working on your own, with a partner, or with the entire class.

1. Interview family members one at a time or together and develop a list of good things about your family. These topics may help direct your questions:

   • Fun things we do together

   • What family members like about our family

   • Strengths of family members

2. Ask an older family member to teach you a family or ethnic tradition, craft, skill, or words in your family's native language. Write a short report about what you learn.

3. Make a meaningful gift for a member of your family. Show it to the teacher before giving it to the family member. Write a brief report stating why you chose that family member and that particular gift.

4. Take a younger relative to the library, a playground, an ice cream store, or another enjoyable place. Use drawings, photographs, or other visual aids to report on the experience.

5. Show your interest in things that are important to family members. For example, if someone had a special meeting, ask about it. Be a good listener. If someone is in a sporting event, concert, or assembly, attend and applaud their efforts. You could also ask questions, such as " What do you like best about your job?" Write a report on the experience and how you think it may have been helpful for your family. Be sure to respect family confidentiality.

6. Learn about a family whose background is completely different from yours—for example, a family from a different ethnic or cultural group or a different geographical region. You could gather the information by reading a book or watching a documentary movie or television show. Write a report answering the following questions:

   • Do the parents treat their children the same way as other parents you know? In what ways?

   • What other important differences and similarities did you discover?

THE WAY IT WAS

NAME: _____ DATE: _____

Use this page to take notes as the guests describe what life was like when they were growing up. Also write down questions you would like to ask the guests when they are finished.

HOME/FAMILY LIFE:

_____
_____
_____
_____

CHORES/RECREATION:

_____
_____
_____
_____

SCHOOL:

_____
_____
_____
_____

QUESTIONS I WOULD LIKE TO ASK:

_____
_____
_____
_____

It takes a lifetime of experience to possess the wisdom of age. —R. R. Sellers

FAMILY INTERVIEW

NAME: _____ DATE: _____

• •

To find out more about your family history, ask a parent or another close relative these questions.

1. How far back can you trace our family?

_____

_____

2. Where did our ancestors live 100 years or so ago?

_____

_____

3. What were their families like at that time?

_____

_____

_____

4. When did our ancestors move to where we live now?

_____

5. What are some traditions that our family has passed down through the generations?

_____

_____

_____

_____

6. Which holidays have always been special for our family?

_____

_____

_____

• •

7. What is a story or saying that our family has passed down through the generations?

_____

_____

_____

8. What are some traditions our own family has created?

_____

_____

_____

9. What is something you enjoy about our family?

_____

_____

_____

Write your own question and the person's response here.

10. My question:

_____

_____

_____

Response:

_____

_____

_____

_____

_____

*The family is our refuge and springboard . . . our link
to the past, our bridge to the future.* —Alex Haley

GROUP PROJECT PLANNER

NAME: _____ DATE: _____

Follow the steps below to plan your group's project.

Names of group members: _____   _____

_____   _____

_____   _____

The skill we will present: _____

_____

STEP ONE

Select a Leader to help organize your project and a Recorder to write down your ideas.

Leader: _____

Recorder: _____

STEP TWO

Think of four or more ways someone your age could practice using the skills included in your topic at home. Your Recorder will list your ideas on another sheet of paper.

STEP THREE

Think of ways you could describe your ideas in a five-minute presentation. Would a skit be helpful? A list on newsprint? One or more posters? A poem, rap, or comic strip? Discuss the possibilities and select one that will interest the class and can be prepared in the time remaining today. Describe what your group will do.

_____

_____

_____

_____

STEP FOUR

Complete whatever preparation is necessary (making posters, practicing your skit, and so on) so your group will be ready to make your presentation during the next session. Describe your part in the project.

_____

_____

_____

TAKING SKILLS HOME

NAME: _____ DATE: _____

• •

Take notes on your classmates' presentations.

Skill: _____	Skill: _____
Ways to use this skill: _____	Ways to use this skill: _____
_____	_____
_____	_____
_____	_____
Skill: _____	Skill: _____
Ways to use this skill: _____	Ways to use this skill: _____
_____	_____
_____	_____
_____	_____
Skill: _____	Skill: _____
Ways to use this skill: _____	Ways to use this skill: _____
_____	_____
_____	_____
_____	_____

Ask a parent or other adult these questions. Record their answers.

Which of these skills have you seen me use?

_____

_____

Which one(s) would you like me to use more often?

_____

_____

The use of riches is better than their possession. —Fernando de Rojas

YOU AND YOUR FAMILY

BY CHARLIE W. SHEDD

Have you ever been in a helicopter? It's a fun ride, slow enough to pick up details you might miss from a fast plane, and high enough to see things you can't see from the ground.

This chapter will be a helicopter ride over your family. It will help you understand your family better and see things you might have missed before. It may even help *them* understand *you!* It describes some basic ideas that have made lots of families happier together.

THE PROBLEMS OF FAMILY LIFE

WHO'S SUPPOSED TO DO THE HOUSEWORK?

Not many people think housework is great fun. Still, most of us have to do it sometimes. By "housework" I mean everything from cooking and doing the dishes to washing clothes and sweeping. These things need to be done to keep a house or apartment comfortable and running smoothly.

Felice and Robert, like most teenagers, think housework is a real drag. Since their parents divorced last year, they've been living with their mother. Before the divorce, their mom was at home all the time. Even Felice and Robert would admit they didn't help much with the housework.

Now their mother works in a department store during the day and sometimes even in the evening. There's nothing she dislikes more than coming home to a messy living room and a kitchen piled with dirty dishes. And there's nothing Felice and Robert dislike more than doing housework.

"She's always after us," Felice told me. Her brother agreed. "The way she goes on," he said, "you'd think that all we're supposed to do is work, work, work! We don't mind if the house is a little messy. It's our house, too."

Who do you think is right? The kids, who don't like to clean house? Or the mom, who doesn't want to come home to a mess? How do you think the family could solve this problem?

Sometimes when there's conflict in a family, the immediate issue (for example, housework) may only be part of the problem. Other problems may be under the surface. In this case, I asked all three members of the family how they were feeling about the recent divorce. Naturally, no one was feeling good about it. A divorce in a family is never a happy event. They agreed that the divorce and mom working full-time placed new pressures on all of them. They decided they all needed to be much more considerate of each other.

Now Felice and Robert make an extra effort to keep the house clean and orderly. Of course, they slip sometimes. The house isn't always perfect. And their mom tries hard not to expect the house to look the way it did when she was home all the time. By trying to understand each other's point of view, this family is finding solutions to some of their conflicts.

TELEPHONE RULES

Who gets to use the telephone can be a problem in some homes, but here's one family that handles it well.

Carl and I were busy talking in their living room when his 12-year-old daughter came in. "Dad, I've got to make a telephone call. This one will take a while. Do you have any important calls coming in?" After her father had given her the green light, she thanked him and disappeared.

I thought that was something special, so I said, "You've got a winner there."

Carl answered, "Thanks, but actually it's all part of our deal. The telephone used to bother us. So we talked about it and decided on a few rules. Everyone had a say. One thing we agreed was that we'd check with each other before a long call."

Carl is a salesman, and he gets a lot of his orders by phone at home. If the kids tied up the phone, Carl could lose some impatient customers. But the family handled it well by making some agreements ahead of time and working it out together.

BICYCLE GENIUS

Juan is a master at fixing bicycles. When he started junior high school, some of his best friends were playing basketball and football, but not Juan. He was taking bicycles apart and putting them back together. By high school he was making his spending money fixing bicycles.

In school Juan didn't study as much as he should have. This was surprising because his father is a high school social studies teacher, and his mother is a guidance counselor.

What kind of problem do you think might arise when parents value education and their son or daughter doesn't? Do you know any families like this? How do they handle it?

Today Juan owns a bicycle shop. No big deal? It is for Juan. While he was still in high school, his parents told him, "Juan, we'd really like you to go to college, but if you want to go to a trade school and learn more about repairing bikes and other things, that's fine with us. We're proud of the way you can do things we can't do. More than anything, we want you to be you." Today Juan's business is growing, and Juan is doing something he enjoys.

Parents get used to taking care of their children and watching out for them. It's hard for them to step back and let kids make their own decisions on some things. Juan's parents were able to do that. But they also made sure that he got the education he needed for the job he wanted to do.

SOMEBODY SPECIAL

Rosemary makes you feel better just knowing her. She isn't a cheerleader or a class officer. She's in grade 7 and her grades are average. Yet Rosemary is somebody special. She's particularly special to Keith. Keith is her brother, and he's in grade 3. Every Sunday afternoon Rosemary takes Keith out for a soft drink or hot chocolate. She listens while he tells her whatever he wants to talk about. It's her idea. Of course, she says it's no big deal. But Keith thinks it is.

Is there someone at your house who needs to be listened to? Would someone in your family appreciate it if you took time for the kind of listening and caring only you could provide?

A NEW FAMILY

Everything was okay for 13-year-old Jimmy until his mother got married again. Up to that point, he'd had a room to himself, and he and his mom got along fine.

Jimmy felt happy for his mom when she started to spend time with Gary. But now that Gary is his step-father, things are different. Gary was part of a package deal that included his two kids. The girl is Jimmy's age; he thinks she's a snob. The boy is five years younger, and Jimmy thinks he's a spoiled brat. Worst of all, now Jimmy has to share a bedroom with his stepbrother.

Many families today include stepbrothers and stepsisters. It's not unusual, but it *is* a change that takes some getting used to. What could Jimmy do to improve the situation with his new sister and brother? What could the whole family do together to make things better?

GETTING ALONG WITH YOUR PARENTS

These are just a few examples of common areas of conflict between parents and their children. Money, chores, clothes, hair, homework, friends—almost anything you mention can become a battleground. This can be especially true in families that are going through stress, such as divorce or remarriage.

When your family is under stress, it's even more important for everyone to think about each others' needs and feelings. Otherwise, problems and conflicts are likely to arise.

As a counselor, I've learned some ways to help families get along better. I've put together these "Twelve Rules for Getting Along with Your Parents."

1. **Remember—you're not easy to live with all the time!**

   If there is one thing as tough as being a teenager, it's being the parent of one. So when things get rough between you and your folks, go look in the mirror. Start thinking about your "people" problems by asking, "Am I the problem?"

2. **You can't always get everything you want. There are other people in the world besides you!**

   You're at the age when you want to try new ideas, feel more grown-up, and impress people. But step back now and then, and try to see the whole picture. Your family wants what's best for you, even if you can't see it right now.

3. **Don't insist on your own way all the time.**

   Don't try to win every argument. Your parents will appreciate it if you give in at times without a battle. Once they know you're willing to cooperate with them, they'll be more willing to cooperate with you.

4. **Show a little sympathy.**

   Trying to understand others is a good start for improving any relationship. Try to see things through the other person's eyes.

5. **Say "thank you" to family members at least once every day.**

   Saying "thanks" will let family members know you appreciate their efforts.

6. **At least once a week, do something nice for family members.**

   Any little thing will do, as long as they weren't expecting it. It's a way to make life a little easier for them. I know one teenager who said to her parents now and then, "This Friday I'm going to stay home and baby-sit. You're going out to have a good time." What do you suppose that did for her parents' feelings toward her?

7. **Never do anything to betray your parents' trust or make them question your honesty.**

   The first time you lie to your parents, you put your foot on a dangerous road. Think of how you would feel if your best friend lied to you. Wouldn't it be hard to trust that friend again? When your family loses trust in you, you have lost a lot. Trust is so quick and easy to lose, but so hard to earn back.

8. **Try to make a few agreements in advance.**

   You can settle some big questions ahead of time. Where can you go? What time will you be in? How much allowance will you get? What work will you do around the house? Dozens of things can be settled in advance. That's easier and more pleasant than arguing about them later.

9. Ask your parents for advice.

You know you're learning more every year. Just imagine how much your parents have learned during their lives! All you have to say is, "I need your help" or "What would you do in this situation?"

10. Ask your parents about sex!

Maybe they did grow up at a time when things were different. But you are proof that they must know a little. If you'd ask your parents, you'd probably learn things your friends can't tell you, because your friends don't know themselves. You could begin like this: "I'm sure you know more about sex than my friends. Will you answer some questions for me?"

11. Learn to talk and listen.

Yelling, pouting, and running to your room in anger will not improve your relationship with your parents. Just as you learn to accept and adjust to your friends, you need to accept your parents and make adjustments for your differences. This will probably require some honest, open talking and listening.

12. Learn how to disagree.

Expect some disagreement. Don't be ashamed of anger. It's a natural part of being a thinking person. The only thing you need to regret is when you handle it badly. Learn how to keep your cool during a disagreement by staying in control and not raising your voice. Don't be afraid to compromise. And, above all, learn these four words: "I'm sorry. I apologize."

Which of these rules would you like to use in your family right away? Some of them may need to be adapted to fit your family's way of doing things, but the principles behind the rules—listening, being respectful, and caring about others—are sure to be helpful. It's never too late to start. Choosing to get along better with your family is one of the most important decisions you'll ever make. Good luck!

. . . .

FACTUAL QUESTIONS:

1. What problem did Felice, Robert, and their mom have? How did they solve it?

_____

_____

2. How is Juan, the "bicycle genius," different from his parents?

_____

_____

3. What are the twelve rules the author suggests for getting along with your parents?

_____   _____

_____   _____

_____   _____

_____   _____

_____   _____

_____   _____

INTERPRETIVE QUESTIONS:

4. How do you think the telephone rules that one family established would be helpful to everyone involved?

_____

_____

_____

5. Why do you think the things Rosemary does for her brother are so important to him?

_____

_____

_____

6. What are some common areas of conflict that arise between children and their parents, according to the article? How can they be resolved?

_____

_____

NO PARTY FOR NANCY

Nancy paced back and forth outside her parents' bedroom door. She could see light under the door, so they must still be awake. Very quietly, she knocked.

Her mother called, "Is that you, Nancy?"

"Can I talk to you a minute?" Nancy said through the door.

"Come on in, honey," her mother said.

Her mother was propped up in bed with a book in her hand, and her father was lying on his side, half asleep. Her mother peered at Nancy over her little half-glasses and smiled. "What's up?" she asked.

Nancy played with the buttons on her robe. "I . . . I just wondered if you and Dad have plans for Saturday night."

"We're going out to dinner with the Jacksons," her mother said. "Why?"

Nancy's fingers traced the pattern on the bedspread. "I just wondered." Realizing how weak this sounded, she rushed on. "Claudia invited me over to her house. I thought if you were going out, you'd feel better if I wasn't alone. I could go to Claudia's."

Her father sat up in bed now. "Who will be at Claudia's?"

"Nobody, really," Nancy said. Boy, was she making a mess of this! "Just a few kids."

"And Claudia's parents?" her mother asked.

"I'm not sure," Nancy said. She was already feeling guilty about not telling the whole truth.

Her father's voice was calm. "Nancy, you know what the rule is. No overnights or parties unless it's been arranged with the other child's parents."

"I'm not a child!"

"You're only 13," her father said.

"Nancy," her mother said, "we'd be happy to talk with Claudia's parents about Saturday night. Just get one of them on the phone."

"It isn't fair." Nancy's voice was shaky. "The other kids are allowed to go without their parents' calling!"

"Is there something you don't want us to know about Saturday night?" her father asked. "Is that why you don't want to call Claudia's parents? I hope not, but that's what it sounds like. Now, there's no point in discussing this any more until you make that phone call."

Nancy turned and left the room. As she walked down the hall, she mumbled to herself, "I never get to have any fun."

As she paused at the door to her room, she heard her mother say, "I hope Nancy's not hiding something. She's never been sneaky before."

Darn, Nancy thought to herself. I did make a mess of this. Now there's no way they'll let me go to that party.

Darn, Nancy thought to herself. I *did* make a mess of this. Now there's no way they'll let me go to that party.

The next morning Nancy got to school early. Standing on the top step, she searched the crowd in the schoolyard for Claudia, holding a hand up to shield her eyes from the sun.

Suddenly she heard a familiar voice. "I know. You're Columbus discovering America!"

Nancy turned to face her friend. "Where've you been? I've been looking all over for you."

"Like Columbus said—I've been around." Claudia grinned.

"Claudia, I can't come to your party. My parents won't let me."

"You *asked* them?"

"Well, I started to, but they told me they have to talk to 'the other child's' parents."

Claudia snickered. "The other child. Your parents are a riot."

Nancy looked down at her feet.

"So what are you going to do?"

"I can't let them talk to your parents. If Mom and Dad find out you're having the party while your parents are away, they'll probably call everybody's parents. Then everyone will be mad at me!"

Claudia took a small compact from her purse, opened it, and inspected her face. "Well, I'm sorry you won't be there. Last night I talked with this guy I know in high school, and he said he's going to bring a bunch of other guys. And some of them have cars. It'll be a blast."

Nancy's eyes widened. "What if your parents find out?"

Claudia snapped her compact shut and dropped it in her purse. "The difference between my parents and your parents is, number one, they won't find out, and, number two, it wouldn't be any big deal if they did."

"You're so lucky." Nancy sighed.

Claudia smoothed her long brown hair with one hand. "We'll miss you at the party, kid. Really. I'm sorry."

Nancy took a big breath. "You don't need to feel sorry for me. I'm going to be there. I wouldn't miss this party for anything."

Nancy spent the rest of the week thinking about going to Claudia's party. She knew it was wrong to go against her parents' wishes. But every time she made up her mind to tell Claudia she wouldn't come, she thought about all the fun she would miss.

By Saturday morning, Nancy decided to try a plan.

Saturday morning at Nancy's house was a time for routines. Her father always did errands. This morning he'd already left the house. Her mother, Nancy knew, would go grocery shopping.

Nancy's routine was to do her chores. It seemed that every year there were newer and harder ones—vacuuming the living room and the stairs, cleaning her room, doing laundry. Sometimes she wondered if her parents spent their spare time dreaming up new chores for her.

Nancy planned to do her chores, as usual. She didn't want things to seem too different. But this was the Saturday of Claudia's party. She would do her chores, but then she had other things in mind.

With the vacuum cleaner running, Nancy watched from her bedroom window as her mother got into her car and drove away. When the car was out of sight, Nancy turned the radio up full blast. Playing loud music wasn't part of the plan, but she was never allowed to do it.

Then Nancy launched Phase 1 of her plan. She rushed to the linen closet in the hall and grabbed two spare pillows. Then she dashed back to her room with them and grabbed her old teddy bear from her own closet.

The two pillows fit nicely under the bedcovers. Then Nancy placed the teddy bear so that its head rested on her pillow. She pulled the blanket over the bear's head and stepped back. Perfect! Anyone who looked in from the doorway would never doubt it was Nancy sleeping there.

Nancy thought about the rest of her plan. About six o'clock her mother would fix something for her to eat and sit and talk while Nancy had her dinner. Then, Nancy would go into the den to watch TV, and her mother would go upstairs. A while later, both parents would come down all dressed up and smelling nice. They'd give her a kiss and a hug on their way out of the house and say, "Be a good girl. Don't stay up too late."

But tonight she would be going out, too. Nancy closed her eyes as she swayed to the music and imagined that a cute boy at the party was asking her to dance. Tonight would be different. . . .

"Nancy! What is going on here! That music is so loud I could hear it halfway down the block!"

Her mother was standing at the bedroom door, her mouth open in astonishment.

For a moment, Nancy just stood there, blinking in surprise. Then she considered falling, sort of, onto her bed so her mother couldn't see what she'd done. But it was too late. Her mother saw. And she could tell her mother understood.

"Turn that radio off," her mother shouted.

Nancy turned off the radio and sat on the bed, staring at the floor.

The silence was terrible. Her mother walked over to the bed and pulled the blanket back to reveal the teddy bear. "Obviously, you didn't expect me to forget my purse and come back so soon. You were going to go to

> *Nancy just stood there, blinking in surprise. Then she considered falling, sort of, onto her bed so her mother couldn't see what she'd done. But it was too late. Her mother saw. And she could tell her mother understood.*

• •

Claudia's tonight, weren't you? There's a party or something going on there, right?"

Nancy nodded.

Her mother frowned and pressed her lips into a thin line. "Come with me, Nancy."

Nancy followed her mother across the hall to her parents' room and watched as her mom jabbed angrily at the buttons on the bedside telephone.

"Hello, Shirley?" her mother said. "This is Ann. Jack and I won't be able to have dinner with you and Richard tonight. I'm awfully sorry, too. We need to be with Nancy tonight. Let's do it another time. 'Bye, dear."

Nancy felt numb. Nothing like this had ever happened before.

"I guess we can't leave you alone tonight," her mother finally said. "We'll talk about this when your father gets home. Now go finish your chores."

Nancy started toward the door but stopped at the sound of her mother's voice.

"Nancy." Her mother's eyes were searching hers. "I always thought we could trust you. I never doubted it."

Nancy just stared at the floor. She couldn't remember when she'd felt worse.

Usually Sunday mornings were fun, but not this Sunday. Almost every Sunday she and her parents read the comics from the newspaper together. They'd been doing it ever since Nancy could remember.

But this Sunday, everyone was in a bad mood. Her parents had decided the day before that they would have to super-vise Nancy much more closely now. Nancy realized that it would take a very long time to rebuild her parents' trust.

Nancy had just settled into her favorite chair when the phone rang.

Nancy's mother went to answer it in the kitchen. "Hello, Janice. Nancy? She's fine. Why? Claudia Morton? Yes, Claudia's a friend of Nancy's. What?! When? Good heavens! Is she going to be all right? Oh, that's terrible!"

Her voice became much quieter. Soon she came back into the room, a worried frown on her face.

"What happened?" Nancy and her father asked in unison.

"That was Janice Phillips. She lives across the street from the Mortons. I guess she knew that Nancy and Claudia are friends. . . ." Her mother sat down on the sofa. "There was a very serious accident last night. A boy had been drinking at Claudia's party. His car went off the road. Several kids were hurt."

"Is Claudia all right?" Nancy's heart was beating fast.

"All Janice could tell me was that Claudia is in Sloan Hospital."

Later that afternoon, sitting with her mother on hard plastic chairs in a tiny waiting room, Nancy decided she hated the smell of hospitals. Finally, a nurse poked her head into the room. "You're here to see Claudia Morton?"

Nancy and her mother both nodded.

"She can only have one visitor at a time, and only for a few minutes. She's exhausted. Her room is 323." The nurse pointed down a long corridor behind her.

"You go ahead, Nancy," her mother said. "I'll wait here."

Nancy got up slowly, half afraid to see Claudia.

Room 323 was nearly at the end of the hallway. Nancy tiptoed to the doorway and peeked in. There were two beds, but one was empty. It was hard to tell who was in the other bed. Most of the person's face was covered by bandages. Then Nancy saw familiar blue eyes.

"Claudia!"

"You think this would make it in a fashion show?" Claudia sounded distant and hollow, as if she were in a tunnel.

"Oh, Claudia! Are . . . are you all right?" "

"I guess."

"But your face! Is it cut? You won't have . . ." Nancy bit her lip.

"Scars?" Claudia sighed. "The doctor can't tell yet."

"Oh, Claudia . . . I wish I could help. What did your parents say?"

"They called me from the ski lodge where they're staying and said my uncle will take care of everything. They'll get home tomorrow night."

Claudia's eyes closed, and Nancy just stood there, staring. She could see tears slipping down onto the bandages that covered Claudia's cheeks.

"I was going to come to your party," Nancy stammered. "I had it all worked out, but my mother found out. . . ."

Claudia's eyes were still closed. "Believe me," she mumbled, "it was a lousy party. You didn't miss a thing. You don't know how lucky you are." She fell into an exhausted sleep.

Nancy stood next to the bed trying to sort out her thoughts. We have to talk to Claudia's parents, her parents had insisted. She'd thought they were being so mean.

• •

I am lucky they didn't let me go to that party, Nancy told herself. I probably would have been in that car, sitting next to Claudia. She looked at the empty bed next to Claudia's and shivered.

FACTUAL QUESTIONS:

1. What are two or three things you know about Nancy's family? About Claudia's family?

2. Describe the conflict between Nancy and her parents. What is the reason for it?

3. How are Nancy and Claudia alike? How are they different?

4. What is Nancy's plan to get out of the house Saturday night? What happens when she gets caught?

5. What occurs as a result of Claudia's party? Where are Claudia's parents?

INTERPRETIVE QUESTIONS:

6. What kind of relationship do Nancy and her parents seem to have? How do you know?

_____

_____

_____

7. Why do you think Nancy's family requires her to do chores and participate in family activities?

_____

_____

_____

8. What are some conclusions you can draw about Claudia's relationship with her parents?

_____

_____

_____

9. How do you think Claudia feels at the end of the story about what happened?

_____

_____

_____

10. What does Claudia mean when she says to Nancy at the end of the story, "You don't know how lucky you are."

_____

_____

_____

11. How do Nancy's parents show they love her? How do Claudia's parents show their love?

_____

_____

_____

FAMILY CREST

NAME: _____ DATE: _____

Draw something in each section to illustrate the five topics below. In the last section, write two words that describe your family.

MY FAMILY AND I

A HOPE FOR MY FAMILY

A FAMILY STRENGTH

OUR HOME

A HAPPY MEMORY

TWO WORDS THAT DESCRIBE MY FAMILY

_____

_____

Focus on the good things in your family.

LOOKING BACK

NAME: _____ DATE: _____

Look back at the list of ways to strengthen family relationships you made at the beginning of this unit. Think about the new skills and information you've learned. How can you use this new knowledge to improve your list? Rewrite your list below, including new skills and information you've learned and adding at least two more ways to strengthen relationships.

HERE'S MY NEW LIST OF WAYS TO BUILD FAMILY RELATIONSHIPS:

1. _____

2. _____

3. _____

4. _____

5. _____

6. _____

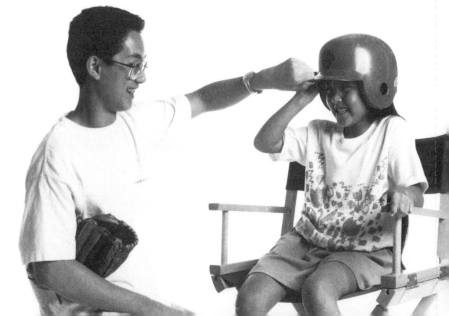

TIP: *Everyone in your family needs love, kindness, and appreciation, just like you.*

NOTES

UNIT 6
LIVING HEALTHY AND DRUG-FREE

Adolescence brings many changes and some major responsibilities. It's the time in your life when your body and mind develop to their full capacity. There's no second chance. If you take care of yourself and stay drug-free, you can become the person you were meant to be. If you miss this opportunity, it'll be hard, maybe impossible, to catch up. Refusing drugs and resisting negative peer pressure are big issues for young people. Several students shared their thoughts about this:

If your friends try to get you to take drugs, then they're not your true friends.

If I were in a situation where others were using drugs and alcohol, I'd refuse. I'd stick to my values and do what I know is right. I wouldn't let peer pressure get me into trouble.

Everywhere you look there's some kind of ad showing people who are cool or glamorous or rich or something, and they're smoking and drinking. But then your parents tell you not to smoke and drink because it's bad for you. I don't know what to think!

It scares me to see what drugs can do to people. My brother got really messed up on drugs. He had to spend more than a year in a special place for people with drug problems. Now that he's out, he doesn't know what to do with his life. He doesn't have anything to take the place of drugs.

It's just incredible that some kids think smoking is cool. Smoking is so gross and disgusting! The smell alone makes me choke. It's amazing the tobacco companies manage to stay in business.

My friends and I have a great time going places and doing things without drugs. We think drugs are idiotic.

I went to a party where some older kids were drinking beer. Some of them were getting really sick and throwing up. It sure didn't look like fun to me!

Why do some people use drugs? They may think drugs will make them feel better—or *be* better. The problem is, people who try drugs are taking a huge risk. They're risking their health and sometimes their lives.

In this unit, you'll gather information about the ways drug use affects your own community. You'll also learn specific ways different drugs affect your body and your brain and keep you from doing your best, right now and in the future. Along with these facts, you'll learn and practice ways to avoid situations where drugs are present and ways to resist offers of drugs. Then you'll help present skits and create a class newsletter to share what you've learned with others and help others be drug-free.

The article for this unit was written by Peggy Mann, a nationally known expert on drugs and youth. "Getting the Facts: Alcohol, Tobacco, and Marijuana" provides you with important information about chemical substances in a way that's easy to understand.

The short story for Unit 6, "Being Cool," describes Angie, a girl who has just moved to a new town. The main thing she wants is a friend. For a while it seems that she's even willing to settle for friends who use drugs. Then she discovers what's really important.

GETTING STARTED

Before you begin Unit 6, write a paragraph explaining what you plan to tell your own children about using drugs when they are your age.

_____

_____

_____

_____

_____

_____

_____

_____

_____

UNIT 6
UNIT PROJECTS

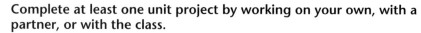

Complete at least one unit project by working on your own, with a partner, or with the class.

1. Write a rap that shares something you learned in this unit, such as the benefits of staying drug-free or ways to refuse drugs. Do your rap for the class or videotape it to show to other groups.

2. Plan a Parents Night, either as part of the Parent Meetings or as a separate event. Think of different ways you can share with family members what you've learned and practiced in Unit 6.

3. If your local cable television company offers free TV time to groups, plan and produce your own TV show to teach others about the dangers of drug use.

4. Develop a list of activities the school and/or student council could sponsor to help students have fun in a drug-free setting. Discuss the possibilities with the principal and/or student council and work with them to offer several of the activities for students in the school or community.

5. Study your school's drug policy. Then think of ways to publicize or strengthen it by helping others realize the reasons behind it. Share your ideas with your class and with the principal and/or student council.

6. Research the drug laws and the penalties for breaking them in your state, province, or city. Invite a law officer to explain them to your class.

7. Research the history of certain drugs. For example, you could explore how small amounts of cocaine were included in soft drinks until doctors finally realized how addictive it is. Write a one-page report or tell the class what you learned.

8. Write an article, letter, or editorial for your local newspaper. Share something you have learned in this unit about drugs or the drug problem, urge the community to offer more drug-free activities, and/or encourage young people to let others know they do not use drugs.

9. Write to your senator or representative (in Canada, a member of Parliament or the Legislative Assembly), explaining ways the state, federal, or provincial government could be more effective in helping young people stay drug-free.

10. Plan a poster campaign for the school or community, letting everyone know that most young people do not use drugs.

11. Organize a poster contest in your school. Select the twelve best posters to be printed on a calendar that also lists school and community drug-free activities. Then you could sell the calendar to raise money to fund more positive activities.

12. Plan and present a program for senior citizens. Invite a doctor to help you stress the dangers of misusing medicines and of combining some kinds of medicine with alcohol.

13. Find out whether any companies or government organizations in your area test employees for drug use. Report your findings to the class.

14. Create a quiz on drug facts. Ask permission to give the quiz to other classes. Be sure to go over the quiz with the students and explain the correct answers.

15. Contact a community-based prevention project in your area. (The Federal Office of Substance Abuse Prevention in Washington, DC, can provide names and addresses.) Ask the director to talk to the class about the project and the school's role in it.

ALCOHOL INFORMATION SHEET

NAME: _____ DATE: _____

DESCRIPTION

Alcohol is a depressant, a drug that slows down the body's functioning. It's made from fermented grapes or grains and is part of beer, wine, wine coolers, and many forms of liquor, including whiskey, gin, vodka, rum, and brandy.

A 12-ounce can of beer or ale contains about the same amount of alcohol as a 5-ounce glass of wine, a 12-ounce wine cooler, or a shot glass (1.5 ounces) of liquor. Each has about one-half ounce of alcohol.

People over a certain age can legally buy and use alcohol. However, it is illegal for people under this age to buy or use alcohol.

EFFECTS ON THE BODY AND HEALTH

How alcohol travels through the body: Alcohol goes down the esophagus to the stomach and intestines. It undergoes little digestion and is absorbed directly into the bloodstream, which carries it to each cell in the body.

The body gets rid of a small amount of the alcohol in the breath, sweat, and urine. The liver slowly breaks down the rest of the alcohol.

BRAIN

Alcohol affects the cerebrum first, slowing thinking, affecting judgment, and dulling senses. Next to be affected are the centers controlling emotions. The person may get silly, angry, worried, or sad.

As alcohol builds up in the bloodstream, it also affects the cerebellum, interfering at first with coordination and reaction time. Then it affects vital body functions, such as the heartbeat, breathing rate, and digestion. Alcohol can slow the brain's functioning enough to cause unconsciousness or death.

Drinking alcohol while using other drugs, especially depressants like sleeping pills and tranquilizers, is extremely dangerous and can be fatal. Many people are hospitalized or killed every year because they didn't realize that alcohol increases the effects of other depressants and other medication, including some nonprescription allergy medicines.

EYES

Alcohol relaxes the eye muscles, making it difficult for the user to focus and see clearly.

HEART

Long-term use of alcohol can weaken the heart muscle, decrease the amount of blood the heart pumps, and produce dangerous changes in the heartbeat. Drinking can lead to high blood pressure. Alcohol use also widens blood vessels in the skin, causing loss of heat.

LUNGS

Small doses of alcohol can increase the breathing rate, while large doses may slow it down.

DIGESTIVE SYSTEM

Alcohol irritates the lining of the entire digestive system. It can cause problems ranging from vomiting to ulcers to cancer. The risk of cancer of the esophagus is higher among heavy alcohol users, especially those who smoke.

The liver suffers most, as it must slowly eliminate 95 percent of the alcohol from the bloodstream, at the rate of about one-half ounce each hour. Drinking more alcohol, exercising, or drinking coffee does not speed up this rate.

If the person keeps drinking, alcohol builds up in the bloodstream faster than the liver can break it down. Drinking very quickly ("chugging") can result in alcohol poisoning and sometimes death.

As the level of alcohol in the blood rises, it increasingly interferes with the drinker's ability to function physically and mentally.

Drinking over a long period of time can lead to a disease called cirrhosis of the liver. The damaged liver cells can't break down poisons, so these substances build up and create problems throughout the body. Cirrhosis is a leading cause of death among alcoholics.

MUSCLES

Long-term use of alcohol can lead to muscle weakness.

EFFECTS ON THE FETUS

If a pregnant woman drinks, her bloodstream carries alcohol directly to her unborn baby. This can cause fetal alcohol syndrome, a pattern of birth defects that may include low birth weight, facial abnormalities, and mental retardation. There is *no* safe amount of alcohol to drink during pregnancy.

EFFECTS ON BEHAVIOR

Because alcohol affects judgment, drinkers tend to do and say things they usually wouldn't do or say. Alcohol also interferes with coordination, reflexes, and reaction time, causing problems in walking, talking, operating machines, and driving. As a result, drinkers often become more confident of their skills, including their driving skills, while their ability to use those skills decreases dramatically.

Some drinkers become silly, while others become depressed, angry, violent, or even suicidal. Alcohol is frequently linked with crime and violence.

DID YOU KNOW. . . ?

HOW OFTEN DOES ALCOHOL INJURE OR KILL PEOPLE ON OUR HIGHWAYS?

Alcohol is not only harmful to young people physically, emotionally, and socially. In too many cases, drinking—or riding with a drinking driver— is fatal. Alcohol is a factor in a greater number of fatal crashes involving teenage drivers than in any other age group. About four out of every ten teenage deaths in the United States occur in traffic crashes.

Fortunately, each year fewer and fewer young people drink and drive. In the United States in 1982, about one in three 15- to 17-year-olds involved in fatal crashes had been drinking. By 1989 that number had dropped to about one in five.

Still, nearly half the total number of car crashes and six out of ten fatal crashes in the United States involve a driver who has been drinking. In Canada, half of the drivers killed in crashes had been drinking, although that percentage may also be decreasing.

A fatal alcohol-related crash occurs about every 20 minutes in the United States. The number of people in the United States killed in car crashes involving alcohol is higher than the number of United States soldiers killed in the Revolutionary War, Civil War, Spanish-American War, World Wars I and II, Korean War, and Vietnam War combined.

In the United States about 22,000 people die in these crashes every year. In 1987, 4,800 passengers riding with drinking drivers were killed. And every year more than 1,800 Canadians are killed and 56,000 are injured.

WHAT ARE SOME OTHER WAYS ALCOHOL CAN HARM OR KILL PEOPLE?

Alcohol doesn't just cause deaths on the highway. At least 3 out of every 100 deaths in the United States and 6 out of every 100 deaths in Canada are related to the use of alcohol. This includes people who die from cirrhosis, heart disease, suicides, car crashes and other accidents, and other alcohol-related causes.

In the United States, alcohol is involved in more than 55 percent of arrests, 70 percent of murders and violent crimes, 20 to 36 percent of suicide attempts, 80 percent of spouse abuse, 48 percent of serious burns, 26 percent of fire deaths, and 38 percent of drownings.

FROM ABSTINENCE TO ALCOHOLISM

NAME: _____ DATE: _____

Fill in the blanks as you listen to your teacher.

ABSTINENCE

1. People who abstain from alcohol _____ drink.

SOCIAL DRINKING

1. How many adults out of every 100 in the United States and Canada drink only small amounts

   occasionally? _____

2. One way that adult social drinkers could suffer long-term harm from their drinking: _____

   _____

3. One of the reasons why young people cannot and should not try to drink socially: _____

   _____

ALCOHOL ABUSE

1. Two of the many problems adults face when they abuse alcohol:

   A. _____

   B. _____

2. True or false? People who abuse alcohol are not necessarily physically dependent on alcohol. _____

3. Because using alcohol is illegal for young people and can harm them physically, socially, and

   emotionally, any alcohol use by young people is actually _____ .

ALCOHOLISM

1. Alcoholism probably has genetic factors. This means the tendency to develop a dependence on alcohol

   can be _____ .

2. True or false? Although children of alcoholics have a higher risk of developing a dependence on

   alcohol, most do not become alcoholic. _____

3. True or false? Most alcoholics have parents who are also alcoholic. _____

. . . .

4. Fill in the blanks with the words that describe the signs of alcoholism:

| blackouts | craving | tolerance |
| denial | withdrawal | control |

A. _____ for alcohol, which means the alcoholic thinks about drinking much of the time

B. A loss of _____ over the amount he or she drinks

C. _____ , which means the alcoholic must drink more and more to get the same effect

D. _____ , which means the alcoholic is unable to recognize that using alcohol has become a problem

E. _____ , which means the alcoholic feels physically sick when he or she stops drinking

F. _____ , which mean periods when the alcoholic can't remember what happened

5. Two other terms that describe alcoholism:

A. C _____   D _____

B. A _____

STEPS TO RECOVERY

NAME: _____ DATE: _____

• •

Fill in the blanks as you listen to your teacher explain the treatment for drinking problems.

INTERVENTION

1. The reason many people with drinking problems don't seek help: _____

2. Here are two people a young person could talk to if he or she were worried about someone's drinking:

   A. _____

   B. _____

TREATMENT

1. The drinker's _____ is often involved in treatment.

2. A group that helps people stop drinking and learn to live without alcohol: _____

3. Two support groups for families and children of alcoholics:

   A. Al- _____

   B. Ala _____

AFTERCARE

1. Two things that will help an alcoholic avoid drinking:

   A. _____

   B. _____

2. Because alcoholism is a physical reaction to alcohol, alcoholics must _____.

3. For an alcoholic, recovery continues _____

   _____.

SOURCES OF HELP

FOR ALCOHOLISM AND OTHER KINDS OF
DEPENDENCE

• •

**Your teacher will give you phone numbers and information to write
in the blank spaces.**

Alcoholics Anonymous (AA): _____

This group helps people who want to stop drinking.

Al-Anon: _____

This group offers help and support for families and friends of alcoholics.

Alateen: _____

This group offers help and support for older children and teenagers
from alcoholic families.

Alcohol Hotline: _____

Cocaine Hotline: _____

Narcotics Anonymous: _____

This group offers help and support for recovering drug addicts.

Families Anonymous: _____

Help for family members of substance abusers

Our school counselor or nurse's name and location:

_____

_____

Treatment or counseling services in our area:

Name: _____

Address: _____

_____

Phone: _____

Name: _____

Address: _____

_____

Phone: _____

TOBACCO INFORMATION SHEET

NAME: _____ DATE: _____

Read the information given for your assigned topic and write one convincing reason not to use tobacco.

1. **INGREDIENTS CIGARETTE COMMERCIALS DON'T TALK ABOUT**
Each time a smoker lights up, more than 3000 poisonous substances enter the body. When the smoker exhales, about 90 percent of the substances stay inside. This includes cancer-causing tars, the addictive drug nicotine, and the poisonous gas carbon monoxide, which takes the place of oxygen in the blood. Smokers have to breathe in more air to get enough oxygen for the body to maintain the necessary balance.

2. **MATTERS OF THE HEART**
As soon as nicotine, the main drug in tobacco, reaches the bloodstream, the heart speeds up and beats an extra 10 to 25 times a minute. Because nicotine also narrows the blood vessels, increasing the smoker's blood pressure, smokers have a much greater chance of heart attacks and strokes than nonsmokers.

3. **GETTING HOOKED**
Almost everyone who uses tobacco eventually becomes addicted. The nicotine in tobacco is one of the most addictive drugs known. It reaches the brain in just a few seconds, making chemical changes and causing a craving for more. Once addicted, a smoker is very uncomfortable when the effects of the drug wear off.

4. **TARS, LUNGS, AND BREATHING**
A smoker inhales sticky tars that are powerful cancer-causing agents. These tars coat the lungs' tiny air sacs, eventually causing them to lose their elasticity and making breathing difficult. A pack-a-day smoker inhales but doesn't exhale a full cup of tar a year.

5. **THAT HACKING COUGH**
Smoking just one cigarette can stop the action of the cilia for 20 minutes or more. These are the tiny hairs in the air passages to the lungs that sweep mucus, dirt, and germs from inhaled air out of the body. Eventually smoking destroys the cilia. Then the only way a smoker can clear out the air passages is to cough, and cough, and cough.

6. **LOSING ONE'S SENSES**
Smokers can eventually lose some of their sense of taste and smell. This happens so slowly they may hardly notice. After a while smokers aren't able to smell and taste the things they once could.

(continued on page 155)

7. RAISING THE RISKS

Compared to nonsmokers, smokers have much higher risks of diseases such as cancer, heart disease, emphysema, gum disease, chronic bronchitis, ulcers, and allergies. The more someone smokes, the higher the risk. When people quit smoking their health usually improves, although many of the damages from smoking are permanent.

8. THAT SMOKER LOOK

Smoking stains the teeth and fingers and can cause early aging of the skin. Because smokers' skin doesn't get enough oxygen, they can develop a condition known as *cigarette face.* Deep wrinkles form around the corners of the mouth and eyes. The skin can look gray or yellow.

9. THAT SMOKER SMELL

Smokers often have stale breath and clothes that smell of smoke. Because the chemicals in tobacco irritate the soft tissues in the mouth, people who smoke or chew tobacco may have gum problems that also contribute to bad breath.

10. RUNNING BEHIND

Research shows that most smokers are not as physically fit as nonsmokers. Because smokers' blood carries less oxygen and their hearts work harder, they tire more easily, cough more often, and quickly run out of breath.

11. FIGHTING FOR BREATH

Cigarette smoke can cause emphysema, a disease that makes it harder and harder to breathe. As the tars from cigarette smoke build up on the tiny air sacs in the lungs, the sacs lose their elasticity. Since these sacs can't be repaired or replaced, people with emphysema spend the rest of their lives gasping for breath.

12. TAKING CHANCES WITH CANCER

Lung cancer is 25 times more common in smokers than in people who have never smoked. It's caused by tars that irritate the lung tissues until they become cancerous. The younger people are when they begin to smoke, the greater their risk of developing cancer later in life.

13. NONSMOKERS BEWARE

Smokers put other people's health at risk, too. Studies show that nonsmoking wives of smoking husbands are three and one-half times more likely to develop lung cancer because of the secondhand smoke they breathe.

(continued on page 156)

14. BREATHING SOMEONE ELSE'S SMOKE

Smoke can bother nonsmokers by making their eyes itch, making them cough, and causing headaches and allergic reactions. Children who live with smokers are more likely to have colds, earaches, and bronchitis—especially when they're very young.

15. SMOKING FOR TWO

A pregnant woman who smokes brings both nicotine and carbon monoxide into the bloodstream of her unborn baby. As a result, her baby may be born with low birth weight, birth defects, breathing difficulties, or learning problems.

16. THE HIGH COST OF HIRING A SMOKER

Smokers may have more trouble finding a job. Employers know that smokers are much more likely to need health care than nonsmokers. They also have more accidents, receive more disability payments, and miss more work than people who don't smoke.

17. UP IN SMOKE

Much of a smoker's money goes up in smoke. Buying cigarettes every day eventually costs thousands of dollars. Smokers also spend more on doctors' bills than nonsmokers. And when they are sick, they're more likely to need expensive care at the hospital.

18. STARTING FIRES

Smokers may accidentally hurt or kill themselves and others in fires. Many fires at home and outdoors are caused by careless smokers who fall asleep while smoking or who throw away a burning cigarette.

19. DYING EARLY

Every cigarette takes about five minutes off a smoker's life. Smoking causes many early deaths (1,200 deaths a day in the U.S. and about 100 in Canada). It's the single most preventable cause of death. The good news is that the number of smokers is decreasing.

20. CHANGING ATTITUDES

Attitudes about smoking are changing. Smoking is not permitted in many public places. Most restaurants make smokers sit in special places and airlines don't allow smoking on certain flights. Hotels, motels, and car rental agencies set aside rooms and vehicles for nonsmokers, and many workplaces are now smoke-free.

(continued on page 157)

· ·

21. GAINING BY QUITTING

Fewer and fewer people are smoking. Most smokers want to quit, and each year thousands do. Many quit on their own and others use special programs, tapes, special chewing gums, or expert advice. Once they stop smoking, many gradually regain their health.

22. IT'S THE LAW

Because tobacco is so harmful, it's illegal to sell cigarettes to people under the age of 18 (16 in some places). In the United States, cigarette advertisements are not allowed on television and radio, and printed ads and all tobacco packages must carry a warning about the dangers of smoking. In Canada, cigarette ads of any kind have been illegal since 1988.

23. NO "SAFE" TOBACCO!

Even though tobacco companies talk about chewing tobacco as being "safe," this is not true. In fact, more nicotine gets into the body from chewing tobacco than from smoking. Users can quickly become addicted and can have even more trouble quitting than smokers do.

24. WHERE TROUBLE BEGINS

Many studies show a strong link between smokeless tobacco and mouth cancers. Many young users have sores, ulcers, and blisters that can develop into cancers. A common place for a cancer to start is on the inside of the mouth in the spot where the tobacco is held.

25. GETTING THROUGH THE TEENS

The longer someone uses any kind of tobacco, the tougher it is to quit—and the greater the damage. That's why it's better never to start. Those who make it through their teen years without starting will probably never take up the habit.

LOOKING AT MESSAGES— PART I

NAME: _____ DATE: _____

• •

Read these descriptions and answer the questions.

PRO-DRUG INFLUENCES AT WORK

1. A poster shows a champion tennis player smashing a ball over the net. The poster includes the name of a cigarette company.

  • What's the poster's message? _____

  • Why is this cigarette company giving you this message? _____

  _____

  • What facts do you know about smoking and athletics? _____

  _____

  _____

2. A friend pressures you to try a cigarette because "everybody smokes."

  • What's the friend's message? _____

  • Why do you think your friend is giving you this message? _____

  _____

  • What facts do you know about "everybody smoking"? _____

  _____

  _____

3. A lonely neighbor offers beer to children who come to visit.

  • What's the neighbor's message? _____

  • Why do you think the neighbor is giving children this message? _____

  _____

  • What facts do you know about the effects of alcohol on young people? _____

  _____

  _____

LOOKING AT MESSAGES— PART II

NAME: _____ DATE: _____

• •

Write as many ideas as you can under each category below.

DRUG-FREE INFLUENCES AT WORK

WAYS INDIVIDUALS CAN INFLUENCE OTHER PEOPLE NOT TO USE DRUGS:

1. _____

_____

2. _____

_____

3. _____

_____

4. _____

_____

WAYS GROUPS CAN INFLUENCE OTHER PEOPLE NOT TO USE DRUGS:

1. _____

_____

2. _____

_____

3. _____

_____

4. _____

_____

ADVERTISING TECHNIQUES

NAME: _____ DATE: _____

Take notes as your class discusses these techniques. Be sure to include examples of the techniques.

TESTIMONIAL

_____
_____
_____

SNOB APPEAL

_____
_____
_____

FRIENDSHIP/HAVING FUN

_____
_____
_____

FITNESS AND HEALTH

_____
_____
_____

TAKING A RISK

_____
_____
_____

JUST PLAIN FOLKS

_____
_____
_____

BANDWAGON

_____
_____
_____

Using the ASK Process

NAME: _____ DATE: _____

Fill in the missing information.

ASK QUESTIONS.

List two questions asked in class or that you might ask:

1. _____

2. _____

SAY **NO** TO NEGATIVE PRESSURE.

List two ways to avoid your group's situation and decide which two group members will share them with the class:

1. _____

Group member assigned: _____

2. _____

Group member assigned: _____

KNOW DRUG-FREE ACTIVITIES TO SUGGEST INSTEAD.

List two drug-free activities and assign them to two group members to share with the class:

1. _____

Group member assigned: _____

2. _____

Group member assigned: _____

WHAT TO SAY: REFUSAL TECHNIQUES

NAME: _____ DATE: _____

· ·

As your teacher explains each technique, write examples in the spaces below. Add your own examples, too.

SIMPLY SAY "NO."

_____

_____

_____

SAY NOTHING, JUST LEAVE.

_____

_____

_____

GIVE A REASON.

_____

_____

_____

CHANGE THE SUBJECT.

_____

_____

_____

USE HUMOR.

_____

_____

_____

ASSUME THE OTHER PERSON KNOWS BETTER.

_____

_____

_____

STICK TOGETHER.

_____

_____

_____

DON'T FORGET TO SUGGEST A HEALTHY, POSITIVE ACTIVITY TO DO INSTEAD!

WHAT MANY PEOPLE DON'T KNOW ABOUT MARIJUANA

NAME: _____ DATE: _____

• •

Take turns reading aloud these facts about marijuana.

1. Marijuana contains over 400 chemicals. When the drug is smoked, these chemicals are converted into more than 2000 chemicals, with even more cancer-causing ingredients than cigarettes.

2. One chemical in marijuana, THC, seeps into the fat-containing part of cell membranes and is released very slowly. A marijuana user's body is still affected by the drug long after he or she has stopped using.

3. THC builds up and can eventually kill the cells. THC tends to collect in the brain, lungs, and reproductive organs and can cause serious permanent damage.

4. Smoking two marijuana cigarettes a week for six months can completely saturate the fatty areas of the body with THC, killing or damaging cells, including brain cells, so they no longer function normally.

5. As THC builds up in the brain, users can have trouble remembering things, making decisions, and carrying out complicated tasks.

6. Marijuana users are likely to get behind in school work and have trouble learning because marijuana reduces their motivation and ability to concentrate.

7. Marijuana slows down the user's coordination and reaction time for four to six hours after smoking. That's why marijuana users are such dangerous drivers.

8. Today marijuana has a much higher THC content and is ten times more powerful than it was in the past.

9. Those who use marijuana can become dependent on it, making it more and more difficult to think and act normally. Others begin to notice these changes, but users usually don't think they have a problem.

10. Two marijuana joints can cause as much damage to the lungs as 20 cigarettes. A marijuana smoker inhales three to four times more carbon monoxide and five to ten times more tar than a cigarette smoker.

11. Those who smoke marijuana *and* tobacco increase the harmful effects of both. That's why they're likely to cough up mucus and blood.

12. Marijuana users are often sick because the drug damages the immune system that helps protect them from disease.

(continued on page 164)

13. Many young men who use marijuana do not have well-developed muscles, do not grow normally, and have less facial and body hair than nonusers.

14. Marijuana can damage the egg cells in a female and the sperm in the male, increasing the risk of birth defects in babies born to users.

15. Smoking marijuana immediately increases the heartbeat and blood pressure. This is a special danger to people with heart problems.

16. Those who use marijuana and alcohol at the same time are in great danger of alcohol poisoning.

17. Marijuana effects build up over time. The younger the marijuana user, the more likely it is that he or she will suffer long-term damage and not develop normally to adulthood.

18. Marijuana is illegal. The penalties for selling and buying it can be as severe as those for cocaine and heroin.

CONNED BY COCAINE

NAME: _____ DATE: _____

Draw a line through statements about cocaine that you know to be untrue. If you're not sure, check *The Truth About Crack and Cocaine* information sheet.

"I think he might make it." That's how Chris' mother describes her son now. But her voice trembles when she recalls the past three years.

The problems started when the family moved and Chris switched schools. He made friends with a new set of kids, some of whom used drugs. The first time Chris used cocaine was with friends at Larry's house. Everyone pooled their money to buy a few grams of cocaine. Larry told them, "It's safe as long as you don't use it too often. It won't turn you into an addict like other drugs."

During the following year, the group tried crack along with cocaine. Chris bragged, "I can handle this stuff!"

Larry agreed. "As long as you only take a little bit, you'll be okay." He said he sold it to them, "at cost," and described it as "pure cocaine."

When one friend ended up in the emergency room from an overdose, Chris thought, "That'll never happen to me. Since I'm mostly sniffing the drug, I won't have any problems."

At 16, Chris dropped out of school. When his parents tried to change his mind, he left home without telling them where he was going. He lasted two weeks working at a pizza parlor before getting fired for stealing money from the cash register. That's when he started selling cocaine. "I'll only do this until I get back on my feet," he told himself.

Chris' family found him living alone in a run-down part of town. A school friend had called the family to tell them where he was. "It probably saved my life," Chris says. "I was half-dead."

To pay for Chris to be admitted to a drug treatment center, his dad took a second job. Chris is grateful to be getting treatment. Now he's able to see colors again. In the depths of his addiction he saw everything in black and gray.

THE TRUTH ABOUT CRACK AND COCAINE

NAME: _____ DATE: _____

• •

Read the following information carefully.

HIGH RISK OF ADDICTION

Crack and cocaine are extremely addictive drugs. No amount of cocaine or crack is safe. The addiction process is basically the same whether the drug is sniffed, smoked, or injected. The first dose can be addictive or even fatal.

A cocaine addict may spend $700 to $3000 a week on the drug. That's why so many addicts commit crimes to pay for their habits.

HARM TO THE BODY

The effects of crack/cocaine are outside the user's control. These drugs send the body into overdrive, speeding up heart rate, breathing, and blood flow. This sudden jolt can cause heart attacks, strokes, and seizures.

Crack and cocaine have powerful and dangerous effects on the brain that can change the personality of the user. Long-term use can cause extreme fear, suspicion, and many other mental problems.

After the effects of crack or cocaine wear off, the user is likely to be exhausted and depressed. This feeling creates a strong desire for more of the drug. This is an important reason why users become addicted so easily.

Users who inject cocaine—or *any* drug— risk getting AIDS or hepatitis.

Drug smugglers and dealers often mix cocaine and crack with other substances so they can make more money. The unknown substances often increase the danger of using the drugs.

HARM TO OTHERS

Cocaine and crack hurt many people besides the user. Family and friends are left to deal with the problems caused by the person using drugs. Treatment is difficult, long term, and expensive. Families often have to spend large sums of money helping an addict recover.

Babies of pregnant women who use crack/cocaine can be born addicted. These babies spend the first three weeks of their lives in painful withdrawal from the drug. If they survive, they often continue to have serious developmental problems.

Eventually most crack and cocaine addicts commit crimes to support their habit. Many muggings, robberies, and murders are directly related to crack and cocaine use.

THINKING AHEAD

NAME: _____ DATE: _____

· ·

Select four of the goals you listed in Session 1 and write them below. Then describe ways that using tobacco, alcohol, or any other drug might make reaching each goal much more difficult.

G⊙AL#1 _____
Ways that using drugs could interfere with reaching this goal:

_____

_____

_____

G⊙AL#2 _____
Ways that using drugs could interfere with reaching this goal:

_____

_____

_____

G⊙AL#3 _____
Ways that using drugs could interfere with reaching this goal:

_____

_____

_____

G⊙AL#4 _____
Ways that using drugs could interfere with reaching this goal:

_____

_____

_____

GETTING THE FACTS: ALCOHOL, TOBACCO, AND MARIJUANA

BY PEGGY MANN

I'll do my best in the next few pages to pick out what may be the most important information you should know about cigarettes, alcohol, and pot. But remember, what you'll be reading here is only the tip of a very large—and very dangerous—iceberg.

ALCOHOL, OTHER DRUGS, AND DRIVING

The fact that this iceberg is dangerous is clearly shown in a U.S. Surgeon General's report on alcohol. Most of the things it has to say are cheerful. Because of giant steps in medicine, the death rate is lower for children up to the age of 14 and for grown-ups over the age of 26 than it was 25 years ago.

But in one age group the death rate has risen: 15- to 24-year-olds. More people in this age group are dying today than were dying 25 years ago. What do you think is the main cause? The Surgeon General's report calls it "driving mixed with substances." What are substances? That's another name for alcohol and other drugs. (The second major reason for deaths in this age group is drug-related suicides and accidents that don't involve driving!)

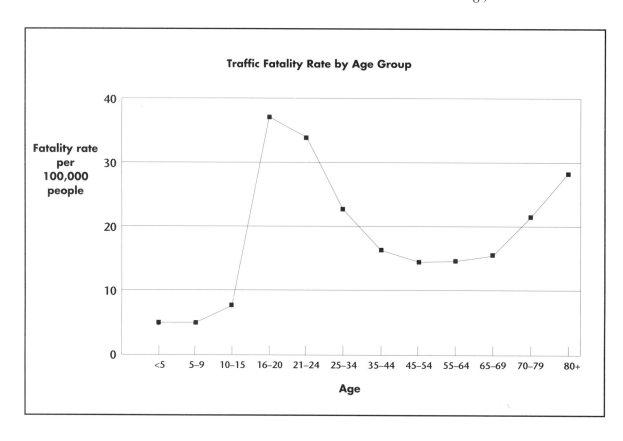

Traffic Fatality Rate by Age Group

Since most of you reading this chapter aren't old enough to have a driver's license, why do I start with the subject of alcohol, other drugs, and driving? Here's why: have you ever ridden in a car driven by a teenager who'd been smoking a joint, or had a few beers, or popped a few pills?

I hope you haven't. But the time may come when someone who is under the influence will say, "Come on. Get in. I'll drive you."

It's not easy to say "No, thanks." But the graph shown here may help you. Do you see how the death rate caused by car crashes shoots up for teenagers? Drivers aren't the only ones killed. Passengers die in these crashes, too.

Some people say, "I'd never ride in a car driven by someone who's been drinking, but I feel safe with a marijuana smoker." You should know that more than 75 research studies have clearly shown that marijuana is just as harmful to a driver's ability to control the car as is alcohol. A driver under the influence of marijuana is dangerous. Many pot smokers also drink, and pot plus alcohol means double trouble.

Half the traffic deaths each year are alcohol-related. The important thing for you to remember is: don't risk being a statistic. Don't worry about insulting the driver. Worry about your own safety, your own life. Phone home and ask for a lift, borrow bus or taxi money, or walk.

Every year thousands of kids your age die in car crashes. Hundreds of thousands are injured. All of us like to think that these things only happen to the other person, not to us. Well, all those kids who were injured or killed in a car crash thought that, too!

Let's look at three substances, starting with one some kids don't consider a drug at all.

ALCOHOL

You already know that a bottle of beer or a glass of wine is a drug. Drugs—at least the kind we're talking about—are mind-altering substances. And alcohol is definitely mind-altering. In fact, that's the reason most kids drink: to alter their minds and get drunk.

On the other hand, most adults do not drink to get drunk. About one-third don't drink alcohol at all, and nearly half of all adults drink only a little—a glass of wine at dinner, a beer during a ball game on TV, a cocktail at a party—but just one. After that they drink a soft drink.

A person who drinks one can of beer gets as much of the drug ethyl alcohol as someone who drinks a glass of wine, a shot of whiskey, or a bottle of wine cooler. All four contain the same amount of ethyl alcohol.

(You should know that rubbing alcohol is not at *all* the same as ethyl alcohol. Some people get confused because the name's similar. But rubbing alcohol is a poison. Drinking even a little can make you very sick. Drinking a lot can kill you, but no amount will get you high.)

Here are other important things to remember about alcohol:

- Alcohol causes more deaths among young people than any other substance. It can alter mood, cause changes in the body, and become an addiction. Because growing bodies are more sensitive to the effects of alcohol, young people are at a greater risk than adults for emotional and physical harm.

- People often refer to alcohol as a legal drug. But it is illegal for young people under a certain age, depending on the laws in your state or province. It was made illegal for a sound and simple reason: to protect your health.

- An estimated three million teenagers are problem drinkers. Alcohol causes them problems of all sorts with school, families, friends, and their health. One of the biggest problems is that they just can't stop drinking without special help.

- Some teenagers "chug" beer—drink it down as fast as they can. This is very dangerous. The alcohol builds up in the bloodstream and can kill them.

CIGARETTES

Tobacco claims more lives than any other drug. In the United States, it kills almost 1,200 people a day. I have a paper from Canadian government and health officials that says 35,000 Canadians die each year because of tobacco-related illnesses. The nicotine in tobacco is one of the most addictive drugs known. The U.S. Surgeon General reports that nicotine is as addictive as heroin or cocaine.

About 50 years ago lung cancer among women was almost unheard of. At that same time very few women smoked. Today, women smoke almost as much as men; young women smoke more heavily than young men. The rate of lung cancer among women now almost equals the rate for men. We know of only one clear reason: cigarette smoking.

Lungs are only one of the organs harmed by smoking, and lung cancer is only one of the ways the lungs are harmed. Smoking has also been linked with heart disease. Tobacco products kill more people every year than *any* other drug, including crack/cocaine.

Pretend that a factory opened up next door to your house and its smoke stack blew polluted smoke straight into your bedroom window. You and your family would soon be out picketing. You'd probably have newspapers and TV covering the story. Everyone would be furious at the factory. Your anger and your message would be heard: "Stop polluting my room. It's bad for my health." But who can hear your lungs, your heart, and other organs when they protest pollution from cigarette smoke?

Alcohol causes more deaths among young people than any other substance.

Even though you won't "hear" the complaints, at least not right away, they're being harmed. The smoke from cigarettes is full of tars and the drug nicotine. With each puff, some of the tars stay in the lungs. A cup a year is left behind in a pack-a-day smoker.

These tars help make cigarette smoking the largest cause of preventable death today. The ads try to make smoking look cool, but medical experts have described it as "slow motion suicide."

A study of 13-to-17-year-olds showed that the cigarette smokers were less athletic than nonsmokers. They read less and got lower grades. They also drank far more alcohol and smoked pot far more than those who did not smoke tobacco. As my 20-year-old daughter summed it up, "More and more kids feel that cigarette smoking is disgusting. And they also feel that being smashed or stoned is tacky and gross."

All of which brings us to. . . .

THE PROBLEMS OF POT

A few people continue to think that marijuana is a harmless substance. Nothing could be further from the truth. There are three main reasons for this:

1. Marijuana contains 421 chemicals. The most dangerous is called *THC*. It harms brain cells, the reproductive system, lungs, and the body's built-in system to fight disease and infections.

2. Sixty-one of the chemicals in marijuana are found only in the *cannabis* plant—the source of pot, hashish, and hash oil. These chemicals, which include THC, are called *cannabinoids*. They are unlike chemicals in tobacco and other drugs because they are *lipophilic. Lipo* means fat. *Philic* means loving.

Instead of washing out of the body as other chemicals do, the fat-loving cannabinoids seek out the fatty sections of the cells. They collect in the fatty organs. The brain, for example, is one-third fat. The sex organs (the ovaries and testicles) are also very fatty.

Very slowly, the cannabinoids leak back into the bloodstream and leave the body through the urine and feces. One of Canada's pioneer marijuana researchers, Dr. Alexander Jakubovic, has pointed out that the cannabinoids take weeks or longer to clear out of the body. If a person smokes a joint a week, the cannabinoids in the second joint add to those in the first, and the body is never drug-free.

3. What does this collection of cannabinoids do? Marijuana smoke brings more cancer-causing ingredients to the lungs than tobacco. Marijuana also has harmful effects on babies of pot-smoking fathers or mothers.

How does this drug affect the brain? One scientist who has done extensive work on pot and brain cell changes is Dr. Robert Heath of Tulane University Medical School in New Orleans.

He divided rhesus monkeys into three groups for his experiment. Some were exposed to pot smoke, and some weren't. After six months all exposure to pot smoke was stopped for another six months. Then Dr. Heath examined the brain cells of the monkeys in the three groups. He found that:

1. The monkeys in the first group hadn't been exposed to any pot smoke. Those brain cells were perfectly normal.

2. The second group was exposed to pot smoke equal to half a joint, two days a week, for six months. The brain cells of the monkeys in this group were beginning to show abnormalities.

3. The third group Dr. Heath called "The Heavy Smokers." These monkeys were exposed to pot smoke equal to two joints a day, five days a week, for six months. Almost all of the many hundreds of brain cells the scientist looked at in this group were abnormal. Some were more abnormal than others. For example, most had dark, swollen clots. These clots are usually found only in very old monkeys or humans. But these were all young monkeys.

When Dr. Heath looked at the damage pot had done to the monkeys' brain cells, he began to understand the symptoms he had seen in many of his human patients who were heavy pot smokers. Their memories were bad. They felt people were out to get them. They were often irritable and depressed. They cared less and less about things in their lives that had once interested them: sports, music, their families—everything except smoking pot.

On the next page is a picture of brain cells from a heavy smoker. One cell was exposed to THC; the other was not.

First, look at the picture on the left. It looks like a perfectly normal cell. The little round blobs hold chemical activators of the brain. These chemical activators must be released into the narrow space between nerve cells to help impulses move between nerves. That's how everything we think, feel, or do is passed on in the brain.

Now look at the picture on the right. The little blobs are all clumped together. This makes it harder for them to release their chemical activators, and it slows down the movement of messages in the brain. It may also affect memory.

Dr. Heath realized that the personality changes in his patients who smoked pot heavily could well have been caused by the same brain cell abnormalities. Of course, people aren't monkeys. But monkey cells in the section of the brain Dr. Heath examined are very similar to human brain cells. According to Dr. Heath, it's wishful thinking to hope that what happened to the monkeys' brain cells does not happen in humans.

The good news is that Dr. Heath and others working with "pot personality" patients report that when teenagers cut out pot completely, they seem to get it back together again. Adults also improve. But they often complain that their memory isn't what it was before they began pot smoking.

One thing is certain. Pot is extremely harmful in many ways. Some of the ways may not show immediately. But over 6,000 scientific studies clearly reveal that the harm is going on slowly but surely in many organs of the body.

With all these dangers, it's easy to understand why every year fewer and fewer young people use marijuana. Since 1980, the U.S. National High School Senior Survey has shown an 80 percent reduction in the number of students reporting daily marijuana use.

I haven't said a word yet about uppers, downers, and the other illegal drugs, but I can cover them all in one short sentence. None of them will do you any good; all of them will do you harm.

One simple word will make life much easier and healthier for you if you're offered alcohol or other drugs. So I'll end this chapter with it.

"No."

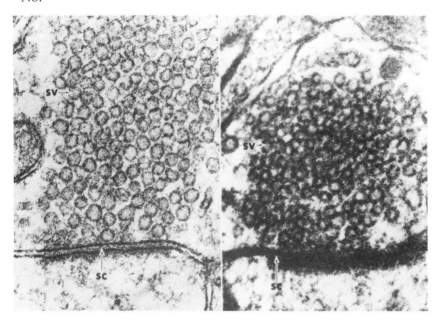

Left: Brain cell from rhesus monkey exposed to pot smoke with the THC removed.

Right: Typical impaired brain cell of monkeys exposed to the same amount of pot smoke with THC.

From *Marijuana Alert,* by Peggy Mann, New York: McGraw-Hill, 1984, p.180.

One of the best ways to avoid drugs is to avoid people who use drugs.

TEAM PLANNING

NAME: _____ DATE: _____

• •

Follow these steps to plan your team's presentation.

TEAM MEMBERS

_____

_____

_____

_____

YOUR TOPIC

_____

STEP ONE: Select a Team Leader to help organize your team's presentation.

STEP TWO: Everyone read the handouts about your topic.

STEP THREE: Assign one or two team members to present each of these subtopics:

A description of these drugs (with examples)

Person assigned: _____

The major effects of these drugs on behavior and health (For teams of four, two people can share this topic.)

People assigned: _____

_____

A summary of the "Did You Know. . . ?" section

Person assigned: _____

STEP FOUR: Practice your presentation with your team. Help each other do the best job possible.

WHAT YOU SHOULD KNOW

NAME: _____ DATE: _____

. . . .

As you listen to each group's presentation, use this sheet to take notes. Use a different sheet for each presentation.

NAME OF THIS DRUG GROUP: _____

SPECIFIC DRUGS IN THIS GROUP:

_____

_____

EFFECTS ON HEALTH:

_____

_____

_____

_____

_____

EFFECTS ON BEHAVIOR:

_____

_____

_____

_____

_____

_____

OTHER KEY FACTS TO REMEMBER:

_____

_____

_____

_____

_____

WHAT YOU SHOULD KNOW

NAME: _____ DATE: _____

• •

As you listen to each group's presentation, use this sheet to take notes. Use a different sheet for each presentation.

NAME OF THIS DRUG GROUP: _____

SPECIFIC DRUGS IN THIS GROUP:

_____

_____

EFFECTS ON HEALTH:

_____

_____

_____

_____

_____

EFFECTS ON BEHAVIOR:

_____

_____

_____

_____

_____

OTHER KEY FACTS TO REMEMBER:

_____

_____

_____

_____

_____

WHAT YOU SHOULD KNOW

NAME: _____ DATE: _____

. . . .

As you listen to each group's presentation, use this sheet to take notes. Use a different sheet for each presentation.

NAME OF THIS DRUG GROUP: _____

SPECIFIC DRUGS IN THIS GROUP:

_____

_____

EFFECTS ON HEALTH:

_____

_____

_____

_____

_____

EFFECTS ON BEHAVIOR:

_____

_____

_____

_____

_____

OTHER KEY FACTS TO REMEMBER:

_____

_____

_____

_____

_____

WHAT YOU SHOULD KNOW

NAME: _____ DATE: _____

As you listen to each group's presentation, use this sheet to take notes. Use a different sheet for each presentation.

NAME OF THIS DRUG GROUP: _____

SPECIFIC DRUGS IN THIS GROUP:

_____

_____

EFFECTS ON HEALTH:

_____

_____

_____

_____

_____

EFFECTS ON BEHAVIOR:

_____

_____

_____

_____

_____

OTHER KEY FACTS TO REMEMBER:

_____

_____

_____

_____

_____

Being Cool

A SHORT STORY BY PEGGY MANN

Angie walked up the stone steps very slowly. It was the first day of school after the summer vacation—which was hard enough. But for Angie it was a triple first. Her first day at a new school in a new town that she hated. Sommerville! For someone who had lived until the age of almost 13 in a big city, to be suddenly moved to a stupid, nowhere place like Sommerville was . . . the end. And here in Endsville she had to try to make all new beginnings.

On the school steps kids were running up and down to greet each other, flinging their arms around each other, all excited about meeting after the summer vacation. Others were going through the school doors arm in arm or standing around in little groups talking. Everyone was with someone. She was the only one all alone.

She entered the school building. The walls were painted white and were brightly lit, a far cry from the olive-green color of her school in the city. But what she wouldn't give now to be walking through those dim, dingy halls—with her friends!

Her homeroom was 3-B. But she couldn't face going in there to spend 20 long minutes until the first period began—watching, as everyone greeted everyone else. She wished her dad had dropped her off just before school started. But, of course, he had to get to his new job at Gardners on time, which had meant dropping Angie off early.

She passed a door that said "Girls" and gratefully went in. At least here it wouldn't show, her being all alone.

Inside the restroom another girl stood by the mirror, brushing her hair. "Hi," she said.

Angie said "Hi" back. Maybe she could quickly turn this new girl into a friend. She took a deep breath and said in one gulp of a sentence, "My name's Angie Bellock. I'm from the city. I'm new in the school and in this town. What's yours? Your name, I mean."

The girl stopped brushing her hair and looked Angie over as if she were measuring her in some way. Then she said, "My name is Gene. Spelled with a 'G.' It's really Eugenia. But everyone calls me Gene—with a 'G.' My friends call me Gigi."

"Oh," Angie said. "Should I?"

"Should you what?"

"Call you Gigi."

The girl shrugged. "Sure." She giggled, though Angie couldn't see what was so

Everyone was with someone. She was the only one all alone.

funny. Then Gigi took some eyedrops out of her bookbag, tilted her head back, and put several drops into each eye. "Thank goodness for Visine!"

She turned to Angie. "Do you party?"

Angie nodded. If she said she didn't, she might lose this perhaps-friend before they even got started.

"I guess in a big place like the city," Gigi said, "they have a lot more fun. I've been to the city a couple of times. It's exciting. Not like here. Believe me, they got the name wrong—this is Deadsville."

Angie nodded, wondering what to say next and hoping she wouldn't make a mistake. "We moved here last week because my Dad was made the new manager of Gardners. He was the assistant manager of their branch in the city. He thought being manager here would be a good opportunity for him. So we moved. Have you ever been to Gardners?"

"Sure," said Gigi. "It's the best clothing store in the mall. You're lucky. Do you get clothes for free?"

"No, but my mom and I do get discounts." Angie started brushing her straight brown hair that hung to her shoulders. Looking into the mirror, she tried to see herself as Gigi might be seeing her: a cool kid from a big city who partied and got neat clothes—at a discount. Except for the clothes, this wasn't who she was. And it wasn't who she wanted to be. But at least it was someone who might attract a friend like Gigi. At the moment, that's what she needed most—a friend.

Gigi was also in homeroom 3-B, and they sat next to each other. Gigi even introduced her to a few other girls. After the morning announcements, Gigi said, "If you want to meet us at lunch period, we hang out behind the shed out in the school yard."

"The shed?" Angie asked.

Gigi nodded. "There's a shed back there where they keep the volleyball net and baseball bats and all that stuff. You can't miss it."

"I'll be there," Angie said. But she wasn't looking forward to it. She didn't like what "hanging out" might mean. On the other hand, she didn't want to walk into the cafeteria for lunch all alone.

Behind the shed meant just what she'd expected. Gigi was there with ten other kids—six girls and four boys. They were passing around a marijuana joint, and several of them were also smoking cigarettes. The teachers who patrolled the yard couldn't see what was going on behind the shed unless they came and looked. And, as Gigi explained, the kids took turns standing by the edge of the shed as lookouts.

Angie volunteered to act as lookout. But Gigi said, "No! I want you to get to know everyone." She seemed proud to be introducing "Angie-from-the-city, whose dad is the manager at Gardners."

The other kids seemed impressed, too. One boy named Joey said, "You probably think we're a bunch of hicks out here in Sommerville. But, hey, the people you see before you are the coolest kids in school."

She didn't like what "hanging out" might mean. On the other hand, she didn't want to walk into the cafeteria for lunch all alone.

Angie didn't know what to say. Her worst fears about this town were true.

"Yeah," said a girl named Sandy. "The other kids call us the 'stoners,' but at least we have fun."

Angie noticed that all the kids—all ten of them—were watching her. And waiting. Waiting for her to take a puff and pass the joint on. She had never smoked marijuana before. She had never wanted to. The kids she hung out with back home never bothered with it.

But this wasn't the city anymore. It was Sommerville—Endsville! Angie glanced down at the joint and finally had an idea. She coughed. "I better not right now. I've got kind of a cough." She passed it quickly to Joey.

Angie felt disgusted. She wouldn't have brushed her teeth with a toothbrush used by all ten of them. And she really didn't want to put her mouth on the wet end of a joint they'd all been sucking on.

When it came around to her again, she wondered whether she should mention her cough again and not wanting to contaminate them. But she didn't want to be classified as a nerd, and to these kids that would be about the nerdiest thing she could say. So she pretended to inhale. Even though she didn't breathe any smoke in, it swirled around her and settled in her hair and on her clothes. She felt like gagging.

"It's good stuff, isn't it?" Joey asked.

Angie nodded, still unsure of herself.

"You mighta thought we couldn't get good stuff out in the sticks," Sandy said. "But we can."

Angie nodded again. They were all watching her, waiting, it seemed, for her approval. "I see." She tried to sound enthusiastic, but somehow the words came out flat.

When Angie got home from school, she found her mother on top of the stepladder, hanging up the living room window drapes. Angie dropped her books on the living room table and sunk into the couch.

"Hi! How was school?" her mother said, coming carefully down the stepladder.

"Rotten!" Angie was surprised at the way the word shot out.

Her mother sat on the couch beside her and lit a cigarette.

"You have to expect that for the first few days. But once you make some friends. . . . "

"I made friends," said Angie.

"Well!" Her mother sounded pleased. "That's wonderful, honey. A new girl in a new school—and you made friends already. You should be very proud of yourself."

"Can I have a cigarette?" asked Angie.

"What?" Her mother looked as though Angie had hit her.

She had never smoked marijuana before. She had never wanted to. The kids she hung out with back home never bothered with it.

"A cigarette, Mom. Kids in this school smoke."

"Kids smoking cigarettes!" her mother said. "Well, you're certainly not!"

"Why not? You do. Dad does, too."

"We'd give anything not to," her mother said. "You know how often we've tried to stop. But we both get so cranky—and I put on weight. . . ." She stubbed out her cigarette firmly in the ashtray. "Just because I can't seem to stop is no reason you should start. In fact, if I have anything to say about it, you'll never take up this awful habit!"

Angie got up. "Well, I've got some homework to do."

"Did the kids smoke in your other school?" her mother asked.

"Some did."

"How come you never asked me about it before?"

"I don't know." Angie went into her room, closed the door behind her, and stood for a long time looking into the full-length mirror on the back of the closet door. She tried to see the image of herself that Gigi and Joey and the other kids from the shed might see: a cool kid from the big city.

Tears came to her eyes. The image in the mirror began to look wavy and watery. That's who she was, really: this watery shape not knowing what to do. Not knowing who to be. Scared of being alone. Scared of getting into drugs. Scared of being called a nerd and a creep.

She wiped her eyes. Then she went to her bed and sat down. She sat there for a long time, thinking. Maybe that's what you had to do. See what you were most scared of and deal with that first.

As she left her room, she glanced into the living room. Her mother was on top of the ladder. Quietly, Angie went into the bathroom and closed the door behind her. In the medicine chest was a row of bottles.

She dumped some of the most colorful-looking pills and capsules in her hand. She could keep them in her purse. Maybe by showing how many pills she had, she could impress the kids behind the shed without really taking any.

"Angie?" Suddenly her mother opened the bathroom door. Angie clutched her hand close to her chest, hiding her pills. "What are you doing?" her mother asked.

She stared at her mother. Then suddenly she began to cry. Huge sobs ripped up from deep inside.

The image in the mirror began to look wavy and watery. That's who she was, really: this watery shape not knowing what to do.

• •

"Honey, what is it?" She put her arms around Angie and they sat down on the edge of the bathtub. Gently, she opened Angie's fist. "What are these for?" But Angie just kept on sobbing. "Those kids in school," her mother said quietly. "They're doing more than smoking cigarettes, aren't they?"

Angie nodded.

Her mother kept holding her, kissing the top of her head until the sobs quieted. Then her mother spoke gently but firmly. "Throw the pills into the toilet." Angie did so. "Now flush it." Angie obeyed.

"Now," her mother said, "wait right here." She returned with her half-empty pack of cigarettes. One by one, she took the cigarettes from the pack, tore each one in half, and dropped the pieces into the toilet. Then she flushed them away.

"I'm stopping!" she said. "I am never having another cigarette again as long as I live. This time I mean it. If someone offers me a cigarette—I'll just say 'No.' Just like I want you to say, Angie, if those kids at your new school ever offer you drugs."

"They already did." Angie couldn't look at her mother.

"Oh, Angie! What did you say? You told them 'No,' didn't you?" Her mother's words came out in a rush.

"I pretended to try some pot," Angie whispered. Then the sobs took over again. "I hated even doing that, Mom," she said when she could talk. "I felt like such a creep, hiding out, sneaking around."

Her mother just shook her head sadly. "We'll talk about this some more when your father gets home."

The next day Angie kept thinking all through social studies about how sad her mom and dad had looked when Angie told them what went on behind the shed. At least they believed her when she said she hadn't really smoked it and never would. And she promised to do whatever she could to help both her parents stop smoking.

Too soon, it was lunchtime.

"Ready?" Gigi had come up behind her in the hallway. She nodded toward the door to the school yard.

"No, thanks," Angie said, trying not to let her voice shake.

Gigi stared at her. "What's wrong? Don't you want to hang out with us?"

Angie felt her heart thudding. "No, it's just—I don't understand why you have to get stoned. And I'm already in trouble at home. I don't need more trouble at school. The teachers here don't know I'm not the kind of person who uses drugs. If they found out about yesterday . . ."

Gigi was still staring at her as though she wasn't hearing right. So Angie kept talking. "Maybe you think you can deal with things while you're high. But I like to remember what I do. I like to keep my head clear."

The teachers here don't know I'm not the kind of person who uses drugs.

"But . . . but what am I supposed to tell the other kids? They'll ask me where you are."

"I guess . . . I guess you could tell them that smoking dope doesn't make them cool, not in the city and not here."

Angie turned and walked down the hall and into the cafeteria. Alone. But somehow she didn't feel alone. She felt together, with herself.

And today, she couldn't wait to tell her mom what had happened at school.

FACTUAL QUESTIONS:

1. Why does Angie want to be Gigi's friend?

2. What are the first clues that Gigi and her friends might be using drugs?

3. What have Gigi and her friends done that is illegal and against school rules? What kinds of consequences might they face if they are caught?

4. How does Angie put positive peer pressure on Gigi?

INTERPRETIVE QUESTIONS:

5. How could Angie have found out why Gigi and her friends liked to hang out behind the shed?

• •

6. What could Angie have done differently when she guessed Gigi might be involved with drugs?

_____

_____

7. Why do you think Angie pretends to smoke marijuana on the first day?

_____

_____

8. What are some ways Angie could have refused the marijuana?

_____

_____

9. Why do you think Angie plans to take pills from her bathroom?

_____

_____

10. What do you think will happen when Angie's mother tries to quit smoking this time? What would have been easier and more healthful for her mother than trying to quit over and over?

_____

_____

SERVICE LEARNING PROJECT EVALUATION

NAME: _____ DATE: _____

· ·

Write the answers to the following questions.

INDIVIDUAL EVALUATION

1. How has this project benefited others?

_____

_____

_____

2. What has been the most rewarding experience you've had as a result of participating in the project?

_____

_____

_____

3. What is the most important thing you learned from the project?

_____

_____

_____

GROUP EVALUATION

1. What are some things you learned that help a group work together?

_____

_____

_____

2. In what ways has the class changed as a result of working on this project?

_____

_____

_____

3. What have you learned about yourself as a group member?

_____

_____

_____

4. The next time you work on a group project, what will you do differently, if anything?

_____

_____

LOOKING BACK

NAME: _____ DATE: _____

• •

Look back at the paragraph you wrote at the beginning of the unit. In it you outlined what you planned to tell your children about using drugs. Think about what you've learned in this unit about drug use and its effects. Rewrite the paragraph, showing any changes in your attitude toward drug use by young people.

Now, what will you tell your children about drug use?

_____

_____

_____

_____

_____

_____

_____

_____

_____

_____

NOTES

UNIT 7
SETTING GOALS FOR HEALTHY LIVING

Recently a number of people your age talked about their hopes and dreams. Here's what they said:

Sometimes I wonder what the future will be like. Who will I marry? Will I be wealthy? Will I be happy? Sometimes I get confused and afraid of what might happen. It's so hard to know.

Some goals I'm working on now are to get good grades, improve my tennis, and get a handle on my very bad temper.

My goal is to learn a lot about cars and motorcycles so I can be a mechanic and have my own shop.

I'd like to lose about ten pounds. I can't do it because I have no willpower.

My hopes are to go to a university and have a good time and start a career. I think I'll have to work hard on grades and saving money.

I don't know what I'm going to be. I'm afraid I might fail or disappoint my parents.

I just want to be happy. I don't have any big plan.

All of us know that happiness and success don't just happen. Almost everyone who has achieved great things has had to work hard. An Olympic runner spends hours and hours of hard and lonely training to get ready for the ultimate test. A rock guitar player has to practice when others are out having fun. Ballet dancers work out daily to stretch and tone their bodies. A good student puts in extra effort to make top grades.

"What do I want from life?" "What am I going to be?" These are among the most important questions you can ask yourself. If you don't, you can end up drifting through life, like a leaf blown by the wind. On the other hand, you can set goals for yourself and work to reach them. That's what this unit is all about.

You'll listen to a panel of adults from your community explain how they've achieved many different kinds of success. You'll think about your role models—and maybe add some new ones. In this unit you'll learn an organized way to set and reach goals. These goals could range from earning extra money to learning a new skill. The activities and discussions will help you deal with the normal disappointments of working toward a goal.

W. Clement Stone, a successful businessman, is an expert on how to set goals and reach them. His article, "Looking Forward: Setting and Achieving Goals," offers many ideas about how you can get where you want to go in life.

In the short story for this unit, "Time to Heal," Jeremy has had a serious injury. The only way he'll be able to walk again is to work hard and keep hoping. But he finds that hope is in short supply—until he realizes that even serious problems can be overcome if you have goals.

GETTING STARTED

Read the three opinions below. Select the one you agree with most. If you don't totally agree with this opinion, explain what parts you disagree with.

Opinion 1: It doesn't make sense for young people to set goals. There are too many things you can't control. You should just wait and see what happens in your life without trying to plan ahead.

Opinion 2: You should set goals and try to reach them. If you run into problems, though, you ought to give up and set a different goal. Keep changing goals until you find one you can reach.

Opinion 3: You should find out what your friends want to do with their lives and set the same goals. You can work toward them together.

I agree with Opinion _____ most. Here are the reasons why: _____

_____

_____

_____

_____

Here's how I disagree with the opinion I wrote about above: _____

_____

_____

_____

UNIT 7
Unit Projects

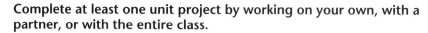

Complete at least one unit project by working on your own, with a partner, or with the entire class.

1. Interview an older relative, neighbor, or friend. Ask the questions below, plus any others you think are important. Write a brief report describing what you learned.
   - What has brought you the greatest success in life?
   - What is one thing you'd like to tell younger people about successful living?

2. Read a biography or watch a film about one of your positive role models. Answer these questions:
   - How does this person measure success?
   - How did he or she become successful?
   - Which of this person's characteristics would you like to develop?
   - What have you learned about success from researching this person?

3. Check with your local parks and recreation department to see if it (or another organization) offers an obstacle course or outdoor adventure program. It may involve such activities as a ropes course, wall climbing, rappelling, and other fun and challenging things. Participants learn to deal with uncomfortable emotions, help each other overcome fears, and conquer what seem to be huge obstacles. Go through the course and write a brief report about the experience.

4. Create a short story, comic strip, skit, or art project that focuses on someone who succeeds in doing something difficult and important. Cover these issues:
   - What was the person's goal?
   - What kind of planning did the person do?
   - What skills were needed?
   - What problems had to be overcome?
   - How did the person accomplish this?
   - What were the benefits of attaining the goal?

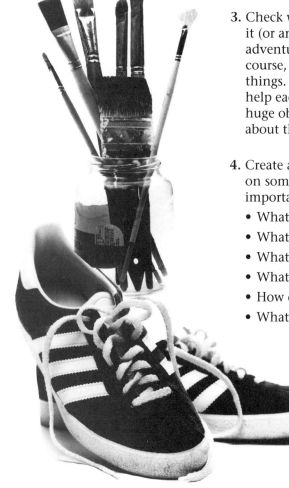

SORTING OUT GOALS

NAME: _____ DATE: _____

• •

List your goals from earlier worksheets under the appropriate headings. Add other short-term or long-term goals you are working toward or want to reach.

MY SHORT-TERM GOALS:

1. _____

2. _____

3. _____

4. _____

5. _____

6. _____

7. _____

MY LONG-TERM GOALS:

1. _____

2. _____

3. _____

4. _____

5. _____

6. _____

7. _____

LIFE PATH

NAME: _____ DATE: _____

Write each of your goals from the *Sorting Out Goals* worksheet on the "Life Path" below, showing approximately when you hope to achieve it.

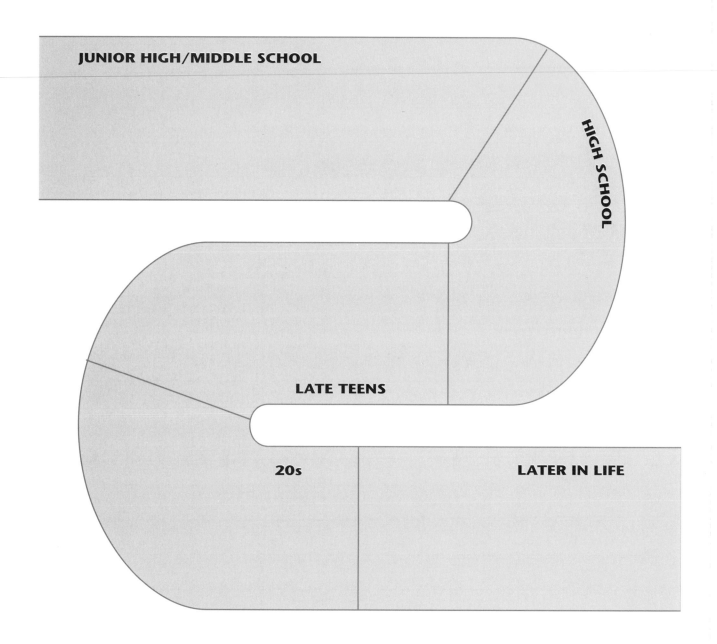

JUNIOR HIGH/MIDDLE SCHOOL

HIGH SCHOOL

LATE TEENS

20s

LATER IN LIFE

POSITIVE ROLE MODELS

NAME: _____ DATE: _____

• •

Ask your partner the following questions.

1. Who is one of your positive role models?

_____

2. What do you admire about this person? What are some of his or her positive accomplishments or characteristics?

_____

_____

_____

_____

3. How has this person affected the lives of others?

_____

_____

_____

_____

4. What goals do you think this person has (or had) set?

_____

_____

_____

_____

5. How does this person demonstrate positive values, such as caring for others, being responsible, being drug-free, and so on?

_____

_____

_____

_____

EVERYDAY HEROES

NAME: _____ DATE: _____

Interview someone who has done something "heroic." This could range from helping someone in need to resisting negative peer pressure.

1. Describe what the person did that required heroism, courage, or determination:

_____

_____

_____

_____

Ask the person these questions:

2. What are some things that helped you in this accomplishment?

_____

_____

_____

_____

3. Did you ever doubt you would succeed? Why or why not?

_____

_____

_____

_____

4. How did you feel when you reached your goal?

_____

_____

5. What would you recommend to others in this position?

_____

_____

_____

_____

INTERVIEW WITH SUCCESSFUL PEOPLE

NAME: _____ DATE: _____

· ·

To interview the guests on the panel, ask these questions as well as those you wrote for homework.

GUEST'S NAME: _____

1. How would you define *success?*

_____

_____

_____

2. What kinds of success have you had in your life?

_____

_____

_____

3. How has setting goals helped you achieve this success?

_____

_____

_____

4. What kinds of achievement are most important to you?

_____

_____

_____

5. Other notes on this guest:

_____

_____

_____

GUEST'S NAME: _____

1. How would you define *success?*

_____

_____

_____

2. What kinds of success have you had in your life?

_____

_____

_____

3. How has setting goals helped you achieve this success?

_____

_____

_____

4. What kinds of achievement are most important to you?

_____

_____

_____

5. Other notes on this guest:

_____

_____

_____

GUEST'S NAME: _____

1. How would you define *success?*

_____

_____

_____

2. What kinds of success have you had in your life?

_____

_____

_____

3. How has setting goals helped you achieve this success?

_____

_____

_____

4. What kinds of achievement are most important to you?

_____

_____

_____

• •

5. Other notes on this guest:

_____

_____

_____

GUEST'S NAME: _____

1. How would you define _success?_

_____

_____

_____

2. What kinds of success have you had in your life?

_____

_____

_____

3. How has setting goals helped you achieve this success?

_____

_____

_____

4. What kinds of achievement are most important to you?

_____

_____

_____

5. Other notes on this guest:

_____

_____

_____

GROWING BY SETTING GOALS

NAME: _____ DATE: _____

Apply the four-step goal-setting process to your group's situation.

Define the goal: _____

_____

Outline the steps to achieve it:

1. _____

2. _____

3. _____

Consider the possible blocks and ways of dealing with them:

BLOCKS	SOLUTIONS
_____	_____
_____	_____
_____	_____
_____	_____
_____	_____

Mark the timeline below to show when you will reach each step and when you will meet a final deadline.

NOW   DEADLINE

⟵————————————————————————⟶

YOU CAN DO IT–
SHORT-TERM GOAL

NAME: _____ DATE: _____

• •

Fill in the information below.

Set a realistic short-term goal. What do you want to achieve?

_____

Outline the steps to achieve it:

1. _____

2. _____

3. _____

Consider the possible blocks and ways of dealing with them:

BLOCKS	SOLUTIONS

Mark the timeline below to
show when you will reach
each step and when you will
meet a final deadline.

NOW   DEADLINE

← ————————————————————————————————————→

You Can Do It—
Long-Term Goal

NAME: _____ DATE: _____

• •

Fill in the information below.

Set a realistic long-term goal. What do you want to achieve?

_____

Outline the steps to achieve it:

1. _____

2. _____

3. _____

Consider the possible blocks and ways of dealing with them:

BLOCKS	**SOLUTIONS**
_____	_____
_____	_____
_____	_____
_____	
_____	
_____	

Mark the timeline below to show when you will reach each step and when you will meet a final deadline.

NOW   **DEADLINE**

←—————————————————————————————————→

PITS TO PEAKS TO GOALS

NAME: _____ DATE: _____

- -

Think of two situations in which a young person might face
disappointment or failure in working toward a goal. Write them
below. Then write possible positive and negative responses to those
situations.

SITUATION 1 _____

PITS

Thought _____

_____

Emotion _____

_____

Action _____

_____

PEAKS

Thought _____

_____

Emotion _____

_____

Action _____

_____

SITUATION 2 _____

PITS

Thought _____

_____

Emotion _____

_____

Action _____

_____

PEAKS

Thought _____

_____

Emotion _____

_____

Action _____

_____

LOOKING FORWARD: SETTING AND ACHIEVING GOALS

BY W. CLEMENT STONE

In this book you've been reading about ways you can make the most of your potential. You've been learning how to manage your feelings, make friends, get along with your parents, and stay drug-free. Maybe you've already done some things differently because of what you've read.

All these things are important for you to be successful, but the most successful people learn another skill, too—how to set goals.

Do you have a dream for the future? Is it something you're willing to work really hard for? That's what a goal is: something you want very much to do or to be.

Think about what you want to do or be, whether it's tomorrow or ten years from now.

By learning how to set and reach goals, you can make your dreams come true. If you don't set goals, you're actually deciding to do nothing. Every successful person you've met or read about had a Definite Major Goal—every athlete, every entertainer, and every great world leader.

To start thinking about your goals, answer this question: if you could do or be whatever you wanted, what would it be? *Think about it.* That's the first step in setting a goal. You think about what you want to do or be, whether it's tomorrow or ten years from now.

SOME SPECIAL KEYS

Wouldn't it be great if you could reach your goals just by wishing? Of course, life doesn't work that way. Yet some people don't do anything *except* wish for their dreams to come true.

Of course, you may wish for a little while. We all need dreams. But successful people know that just dreaming isn't enough. To make their dreams come true, they need to take action.

I have some suggestions for things you can do that will help you take action to reach your goals. Think of them as special keys that can open the doors of success. They're things you can do to get where you want to go. These keys worked for me, and they can work for you, too.

Here are the first two:

Make this promise to yourself: "I will try to learn things that will help me become the best I can be and achieve success in everything I do."

The skills and ideas you've been learning in the *Skills for Adolescence* program will give you a head start here.

Dream big dreams. Set goals that are really high. As the old saying goes, "The sky's the limit." Aim high!

Why doesn't everybody achieve success and reach as high as he or she can go? One answer is that life is full of roadblocks, or things that stand in our way and keep us from achieving our goals.

One roadblock is fear. Many people fear they will fail or other people will laugh at them. So they don't try hard, or they give up too easily. I know it's not easy to overcome fear. But you can do it! Let me tell you how I overcame a fear that stood in my way.

As a young child, I was very fearful, probably more so than most children. I was so scared of lightning that I ran into the bedroom during thunderstorms and hid under the bed. One day while hiding there, I decided that if lightning struck, it would probably be just as dangerous under the bed as anywhere else in the room. So I forced myself to go to the window and look at the flashes of light.

An amazing thing happened: I enjoyed the beauty of the lighted sky and especially the BOOM of the thunder. Today, I really *like* a good, loud storm.

I overcame my fear and began a new habit that has helped me reach many other goals: I learned how to do what I was afraid to do. This led to one of my favorite sayings: "When you have a worthy goal, do what you're afraid to do. Don't let fear stand in your way."

THE ROOTS OF MY SUCCESS

My father died when I was a young child. Mother and I lived with my aunt and uncle in a rundown neighborhood in the rough, tough South Side of Chicago. Mother worked as a dressmaker. My aunt and uncle waited on tables at restaurants. We were very poor.

As a young boy, I wanted to earn money instead of asking my mother for it. So I decided to sell newspapers. You had to buy your papers in advance, and I borrowed the money from a friend. It wasn't much, but it was a lot to me because I didn't have any.

I went to a busy corner, 31st Street and Cottage Grove, where two older newsboys were yelling out the headlines. I tried to act like them and yelled as loudly as I could. But they shouted, "Get out of here!"

I refused to leave, so they beat me up. I was hurt and confused, and I cried. But I couldn't return the papers. I *had* to sell them.

Not knowing what to do, I walked north on Cottage Grove until I came to Hoelle's Restaurant, which was full of customers. I got an idea. I would try to sell newspapers to the people in the restaurant.

At first the owner, Mr. Hoelle, didn't like the idea, but when I showed him how important selling the papers was to me, he relented. Actually, his customers told him they liked my attitude. One of them even gave me a dime tip! (That was a lot of money in those days.)

After a while, Mr. Hoelle and I became good friends. He really helped my mother and me. We were lucky to know him, for he was generous and caring.

A positive mental attitude means believing in yourself and your abilities.

I didn't realize until years later that my success in the business world had its roots in the many hours I spent as a kid selling newspapers.

"PMA"

Long after I founded my own company, I wrote a book called *The Success System That Never Fails*. As I remembered the days when I worked so hard to sell newspapers, I came up with another key to success. I wrote about it in that book:

 **To reach your goals, you need to have a Positive Mental Attitude, PMA for short. With PMA, you can reach almost any goal. Without it, you may work twice as hard as anyone else and still not succeed.**

A positive mental attitude means believing in yourself and your abilities. It means thinking to yourself, "I can do it. Even if it takes a lot of hard work and a long time, I can do it." PMA is like an engine inside you that keeps you going, keeps driving you on.

How do you develop a positive mental attitude? Here are some tips:

Be more positive. Some people are always putting themselves down. You may be one of them. Instead ask yourself, "What are my good qualities?" (Everybody has some.) "What do I do best? What talents do I have that I can build on?"

Take action. Act to reach your goals. To begin, eliminate at least one bad habit in the next month, such as not doing your homework or eating too much candy or junk food. Keep a chart of your progress.

Choose friends who share your goals and values. Especially during the teenage years, your friends influence what you do and think. Ask yourself, "Are my friends the kind of people who will support me and help me reach my goals? Do I admire the way they act? Do I admire their goals?"

These are just a few ways you can start to develop a positive mental attitude. They've worked for successful people all over the world.

. . . .

A POSITIVE ROLE MODEL

My mother was one of the most positive people in my life. She had a positive mental attitude and always set a good example for me.

When I was a boy she worked at Dillon's, one of the best dressmaking companies in Chicago. But she had a Major Definite Goal—to own her own business—and she never forgot that goal.

 **Think about the people you admire. What positive things have they done?**

After only a couple of years at Dillon's, my mother was in charge of all the designing, fitting, and sewing. She was almost as important as the boss. She became known as an outstanding designer and dressmaker.

Her earnings increased every year. And during those years she gave up a lot by saving part of her salary to achieve her goal. Finally, after six years at Dillon's, she opened her own shop in our new apartment in a nice neighborhood. Now *she* was the boss. And after my mother reached this major goal, she set and reached many more.

PASSING UP A CHANCE

After we moved to the nicer neighborhood, I attended school about six blocks from home. But I wasn't what you'd call a good student. Mostly I got *C's*. I settled for just passing instead of trying for high grades.

I didn't know then what I know now. Had I worked to earn better grades, I would have saved a lot of time and money. Many years later, after I had started my own business, I had to go to night school to learn what I needed to know to get into a good university.

Now I'm able to help people all over the world. But my life would have been easier if I'd known an important key:

 **Don't lose sight of your goal. Keep reminding yourself of what you want to achieve. Take action every day to move in the right direction.**

STORIES TO REMEMBER

When I was a young teenager, my mother sent me to spend a summer at Green's Michigan Farm and Summer Resort.

Exploring the attic one day at Green's Farm, I found at least 50 books written by a man named Horatio Alger. These books were so popular that millions of kids used to read them, just the way kids watch some popular television shows today. I took one of the dusty, worn books to the front yard, lay in a hammock, and began to read. I was so excited by the stories and the ideas that I read all 50 books that summer.

The theme in each book was simple. Each hero was a teenager who became successful by:

- Being honest and hard-working.
- Treating others fairly.
- Doing the right thing because it was right.
- Memorizing and following the Golden Rule: Treat others as you would like them to treat you.

The Horatio Alger books inspired me and many other teenagers to work toward success the good and right way. Here's another key I learned from reading those 50 books:

 **Look for ways to achieve your goals in everything you read and everything that happens to you. That way, you'll always be moving toward your goals.**

ONE MORE KEY

If you want to succeed in life, you need to set goals, look for new information that will help you reach your goals, and put what you know into action.

 **A self-motivator can help you reach your goals. A few simple words can be your guide to success.**

Do you ever put things off? Three simple words can help you overcome that habit. Repeat the self-motivator "Do it now!" over and over again when you wake up in the morning and before you go to sleep at night. You'll be amazed how saying these words again and again will help you take action.

Then if you're tempted to put off something important, tell yourself, "Do it now!" With time and practice, you'll find that "Do it now!" will just come to your mind and you'll form a habit of getting things done.

As you grow older, you'll have more and more responsibility for your own life. You'll be the one who sets goals, gathers information, figures out a plan, and makes things happen. By learning how to set and work toward goals, you'll prepare yourself for a successful future. The time to start is now!

• •

FACTUAL QUESTIONS:

1. What were some of the hardships W. Clement Stone faced as a child?

   _____

2. Describe a time when the author failed at something and decided he had to work harder to do well.

   _____

3. How did the books by Horatio Alger provide role models?

   _____

4. What is *PMA?*

   _____

5. What are the keys that W. Clement Stone suggests for achieving your goals?

   _____   _____

   _____   _____

   _____   _____

   _____

6. What is the self-motivator he suggests?

   _____

INTERPRETIVE QUESTIONS:

7. How do you know the author thinks role models are important?

   _____

   _____

8. Who were his role models?

   _____

   _____

9. How does a "dream" become a reality? Give some examples from the article.

   _____

   _____

10. How does PMA compare to the pits-to-peaks approach to dealing with disappointment?

   _____

   _____

BIOGRAPHY OUTLINE

NAME: _____ DATE: _____

Fill in the information below to create an outline for your biography. Remember that this biography will cover the time from now until your late 20s.

BASIC INFORMATION

One short-term goal I will include: _____

Three long-term goals I will include:

1. _____

2. _____

3. _____

At least one positive role model I will mention: _____

At least one time I may face disappointment as I work toward one of my goals: _____

_____

_____

_____

SPECIFIC INFORMATION

Write the details you will include for each time period. Be sure to show the steps you take to reach each short-term and long-term goal. Also decide when to describe your role model and when to tell how you dealt with disappointment in reaching a goal.

During my school years: _____

_____

_____

_____

During my late teens: _____

_____

_____

_____

During my 20s: _____

_____

_____

_____

TIME TO HEAL

A SHORT STORY

Jeremy should have been working on a book report. Instead, he sat in the easy chair with the cast on his left leg propped up on the footstool, watching TV. Mainly, he was trying not to think.

His mom came out from the kitchen, where she was finishing the dinner dishes. An apron covered the good clothes she wore to her office downtown. "You want some milk, Jeremy?"

"Yeah, sure." But then he quickly added, "Mom, you don't have to wait on me. I can get it myself."

"Don't be silly. I'll get it."

"But I want to do it myself!" Jeremy was surprised that suddenly he felt like crying. It had been six weeks since he had come home from the hospital, and moving still took a huge effort. But he had to do it.

He slid the cast onto the floor, picked up his crutches, and hauled himself out of the chair.

"Thanks anyway, Mom." He managed to get the crutches and the cast through the kitchen doorway. "I can do it myself."

After drinking some milk, lurching back into the living room, and plopping down in front of the television set again, Jeremy closed his eyes. A game show was on. The only reason people watched those shows, he thought, was so they could pretend their wishes were coming true.

Jeremy thought about his own wish. He wished one moment in his life had never happened—the moment when he'd slid into the street on his skateboard and a car came out of nowhere and hit him, crushing his leg. But Jeremy knew wishing wouldn't make a bit of difference. The damage was done.

At least tomorrow, exactly eight weeks after the accident, Dr. Walker would take off the hot, heavy, itchy cast. Jeremy had been counting the days until the cast came off, but he wasn't sure he wanted to see what was underneath.

Jeremy had high hopes things would go back to the way they were. He could go back to being the best backcourt shot in the neighborhood. And the best hitter on the Police Athletic League baseball team. At 14, he had already become the star, the leader.

The next day Jeremy sat with his mother in the reception room, anxiously waiting to see Dr. Walker. He stared at the picture of Dr. Charles Drew hanging on the wall. He was always amazed by how much the two doctors looked alike.

"Jeremy?" The nurse interrupted his thoughts. "Follow me, please."

"Hello, Jeremy," Dr. Walker boomed. "Are you ready for this? It will be completely painless. I promise." He was tall and important-looking. But he was kind, and Jeremy trusted him.

"I want to do it myself!"

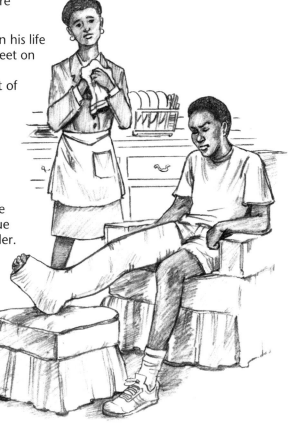

211

"Yeah. Let's get this over with."

Jeremy could barely watch as Dr. Walker sawed through the cast that stretched from the top of his leg to his foot. When the doctor pulled the cast off, the skin on Jeremy's leg was wrinkled and grey instead of its usual warm-brown color. His lower leg was crisscrossed with scars.

"It looks pretty bad right now," Dr. Walker said. "It'll start looking better, but it's always going to be scarred. Let's see how it works. Try to move your toes." He watched Jeremy's foot. "Well?"

"I'm trying," Jeremy said. But nothing happened.

"Try lifting your leg," Dr. Walker said. "See if you can move it just a little bit."

Jeremy closed his eyes and concentrated on lifting his leg. Nothing.

"Hmm," Dr. Walker said. "Try moving just the foot now." But again . . . nothing.

The doctor started to poke at the leg with what looked like a giant needle. "Feel anything?"

"I think so," Jeremy said. "Yeah—sort of a tingling."

"Well, that's encouraging. It means there's some hope for this leg." Dr. Walker put away the giant needle and stood up. "In a way, you're lucky. There's a very slim chance that someday you'll be able to walk with that leg. For now you'll still need crutches. Maybe later on, you'll need to wear a brace. You'll also need physical therapy and time, which together might help this leg work better. But we don't know. We just have to try."

Dr. Walker turned to Jeremy's mom. "I'll give you the names of some physical therapists. They'll give him twice weekly therapy sessions and teach Jeremy exercises he can do at home in between."

Then he turned back to Jeremy. "A lot will depend on you, young man. But you've got a great mom to help you, and you're not so bad yourself." He punched Jeremy's shoulder lightly. Jeremy tried to smile.

Jeremy's mom tried to smile, too. "I guess I can stand him."

Waiting in the hall for the elevator, Jeremy knew his mom was trying to think of something positive to say. Finally she whispered, "Everything's going to be all right."

The next afternoon was clear and sunny. People were sitting on the front steps of the apartment buildings that lined the street, talking and laughing. Teenagers danced on the sidewalks with their radios turned up loud, and younger kids rode bicycles and skateboards.

Jeremy had walked home from school on his crutches every day since leaving the hospital. It was only four blocks. Today was his first day without the cast, but it didn't make much difference. His left leg was as stiff as if it were still covered with plaster. The crutches had become a part of him.

"Hey, Jeremiah! How's my man?" Jeremy turned around at the sound of the familiar voice. It was Mr. Talera, who ran a vegetable market in the middle of the block. For the last two summers, Mr. Talera had let him work a couple hours every day as a bag boy. With tips, he could make $40 a week.

"Hi, Mr. Talera, how you doing?" Jeremy said.

Mr. Talera had a round face with apple cheeks, and he always seemed to be laughing. "Can't complain. And you? You got your cast off. How's that leg?"

"I'm doing all right, Mr. Talera. Thanks." Jeremy moved on. Mr. Talera called after him. "So how long you gotta walk on them crutches? I'm counting on you to help me out again this summer, Jeremiah. You're one of the best helpers I ever had."

"Maybe you better look for someone else this summer," Jeremy said.

"Aw, just give yourself some time," Mr. Talera said. "I'm saving the spot for you."

Jeremy went on. Turning a corner, he saw three boys sitting on a front stoop. Even half a block away, he knew who they were: Tony, Jason, and Oscar. They called themselves the Trouble Brothers.

As Jeremy got closer, the boys stopped laughing and joking to stare at him.

As Jeremy got closer, the boys stopped laughing and joking to stare at him. Jeremy stared right back as he passed. But nobody said a word.

Then he heard Tony's voice. "Hey, Jeremy!"

Jeremy turned around, steeling himself for whatever was coming. "Yeah?"

"You got your cast off, huh?" Tony asked. The question sounded almost friendly.

"Yeah," Jeremy said. "So what?"

"Is it true you're crippled?" Tony asked.

Now Jason cut in. "Some of the guys were saying you'll always have to use crutches. . . ."

Even Oscar, who hardly ever talked, had an opinion. "My mom said your leg is ruined. You'll never do sports or nothing."

"Is it true?" Tony asked.

Jeremy felt a dull, aching pain. Finally he spat out an answer. "What happens with my leg is none of your business."

Back in the apartment, Jeremy dropped into the easy chair. He rested his leg on the footstool and covered his eyes with his hands.

His mom came out of the kitchen. "Hi. How you doing? Everything okay?"

"Yeah, I guess so."

"What happened?"

"Nothing."

"Nothing—and you're sitting there with your hands over your eyes."

He dropped his hands and glared at her. "It's not important."

"Right. I can see that."

Suddenly Jeremy couldn't pretend anymore. "I hate this leg! I hate it!" He looked at the leg, lying there on the footstool like some dead thing, and hit it hard with his fist. "I hate it! Why didn't they cut it off?"

His mom had tears in her eyes. "Oh, Jeremy, honey, don't!"

Jeremy hit the leg again with his fist—even harder than before. But this time he smiled. "Hey! Whooee! Ma, I think it moved. I could swear it kind of jumped when I hit it. Felt like I made it move."

For five minutes Jeremy sat there trying to make his leg move. He even tried hitting it again. But it didn't budge.

Finally he sank back in the chair. "Forget it. It was probably just my imagination. Maybe it didn't move at all."

"Maybe if you want it enough," his mom said, "it will happen. Your physical therapy starts tomorrow. Maybe that will help, too."

"Sure," Jeremy said bitterly.

"Don't give up, Jeremy. Self-pity is a dangerous enemy." For a moment she seemed about to go on with some long lecture, but then she asked, "Son, did you tell Mr. Talera you'd work in his store again this summer?"

"No way! How could I? I can barely stand up!"

All she did was nod.

The next night at dinner, his mother had a surprise. "Jeremy, I want you to come downtown with me tomorrow morning. I think I found a summer job for you."

"I have school tomorrow," Jeremy objected. "Anyway, what kind of job could I do now?"

"I already called your school. You're excused from classes tomorrow. Just be looking your best and ready to leave for the bus at 7:25 in the morning, okay?"

He sighed. "Yeah. Okay." At least it sounded better than another day at school with everyone pretending not to notice he was "crippled" now.

It wasn't easy getting on or off the bus the next morning, but Jeremy managed with his mom's help. They started down the street toward her office, but his mom walked right past the building where she worked.

Jeremy stopped by the door. "Ma," he called. "Here it is."

"That's where *I* work." She nodded toward the building next door. "This is where *you* might work, if they like you," she added with a smile.

He looked at the leg, lying there on the footstool like some dead thing, and hit it hard with his fist.

They went inside and took the elevator up to the fourth floor. Jeremy followed his mother down a long hallway to an office marked "Human Resources."

A receptionist sitting at a desk inside took Jeremy's name and motioned for them both to sit in a row of chairs. "Mr. Franklin will be with you in a few minutes."

"This is a waste of time," Jeremy whispered. "Just wait till Mr. Franklin or whatever his name is sees these crutches."

His mother raised her eyebrows. "I'll wait."

The phone on the receptionist's desk rang. She answered it and said to Jeremy, "Mr. Franklin will see you now." She pointed down a hallway behind her. "It's the third room on the right."

Jeremy struggled to his feet and stood there a second, waiting for his mom to stand up.

"This is your appointment and your job, not mine," she told him calmly. "Go and talk to Mr. Franklin. He won't bite. I know. He's a friend of mine."

"Mom . . . ," He kept his voice low so the receptionist wouldn't hear. "Please come with me." Why was she doing this to him?

But his mother just smiled and shook her head. Jeremy's heart was pounding by the time he reached the third door on the right. He balanced on his crutches and knocked.

"Come in," called a deep voice.

Jeremy pushed open the door and started inside. He immediately caught one of his crutches on the leg of a couch near the door. After he managed to get untangled without actually falling, he looked up. A man with a short beard and glasses was sitting at a desk, watching him and smiling.

Jeremy felt his face get hot. "I'm Jeremy. My mom said. . . ."

Mr. Franklin pointed at a chair opposite his desk. "Have a seat. Let's talk about what you can do for us here this summer."

"Not much," Jeremy mumbled as he lurched toward the chair. Coming here had been a mistake, a real mistake.

"Is that right?" Mr. Franklin asked. "You mean because you need crutches to walk?"

"Well . . . yeah." Can't you see how hard this is, Jeremy wanted to yell.

"Well, I need someone to put together packages of materials when customers call in orders, but I guess I'll have to find someone else."

"Uhh . . . Wait . . . Maybe I *could* do that. Would I have to do any . . . any walking?"

"Some. Is that out of the question?" Mr. Franklin looked Jeremy right in the eye.

Can't you see how hard this is, Jeremy wanted to yell.

Jeremy swallowed, but the man wouldn't let him look away. "No, I guess not."

The rest of the interview went a lot better than he expected. Finally, Mr. Franklin said, "Well, Jeremy, I think you'll do a fine job for us. Did your mom come with you today?"

Jeremy nodded.

"I'll come out and say hello." With that, Mr. Franklin pushed back his chair, but instead of standing up, his whole chair moved around his desk with him.

He was sitting in a wheelchair. When he came around to the front of his desk, Jeremy saw that both pant legs were folded under at the knee. He tried not to stare.

"Viet Nam," Mr. Franklin said simply. "I lost the bottom half of both legs when I stepped on a landmine. I always was a klutz," he added with a smile.

"Oh." It was all Jeremy could say.

A few minutes later, as Jeremy and his mother headed for the elevator, his head was crowded with thoughts. He couldn't wait to start his new job. More than anything, he wanted to get to know Mr. Franklin better.

"Hey!" Jeremy said. "I've got physical therapy today, don't I? Did you know Mr. Franklin goes to physical therapy, too? I don't want to miss it. I've got a lot of work to do."

His mother's eyes sparkled. "You do?"

"Are you kidding? I've got to learn to walk without these crutches. Maybe if I work hard, I can get along with just a brace. And after that, who knows? I may even make this old leg work by itself again."

Jeremy grinned and looked at his mom. "Thank you, Mom. Thanks for everything."

* *

FACTUAL QUESTIONS:

1. What has happened to Jeremy?

   _____

2. How do you know Jeremy is feeling very sorry for himself?

   _____

3. How does his mother react?

   _____

4. What does Dr. Walker tell Jeremy about his leg?

   _____

5. How was Jeremy affected by the other boys' comments?

   _____

6. What happens when Jeremy pounds his leg in frustration?

   _____

7. How does his mother help motivate him to set goals again?

   _____

8. What does Jeremy decide to do at the end of the story? For what reasons?

   _____

INTERPRETIVE QUESTIONS:

9. What kind of person was Jeremy before his accident? How do you know?

   _____

   _____

10. How do you think Jeremy feels about the changes in his life at the beginning of the story? At the end?

    _____

    _____

11. What do you think is the most important factor in making Jeremy want to change his behavior at the end of the story?

    _____

    _____

LOOKING BACK

NAME: _____ DATE: _____

Look back at the three opinions about setting goals that were listed at the beginning of this unit. Reread the response you wrote. In the space below, add to your response, showing what you've learned during the activities and discussions of this unit.

_____

_____

_____

_____

_____

_____

_____

_____

NOTES

SUMMING UP
DEVELOPING YOUR POTENTIAL

Congratulations! You've completed the *Skills for Adolescence* program! What specific things have you learned that can help you become the best you can be? Here are some thoughts from a group of students who were part of the program:

I'm glad I learned more about the changes I'm going through so I know better what to expect.

It helps me to know how to solve problems with my friends so we can get along and support each other instead of arguing all the time.

I've learned how to stick up for myself. Now I won't go along with the group and do things I'll feel bad about later.

I'm sure I'll get more out of my life now that I know how to set goals and work toward them.

One thing I've learned is to ask myself if I'm hurting anyone by accomplishing my goals. I realize now how important it is not to walk all over my family or friends for my own benefit. I think I've learned how to be a better person.

Learning how to say "No" to alcohol and other drugs is the most important thing to me because they can mess you up.

Listening to people—really listening—is a big part of making and keeping friends. And friends are very important.

I think the most important thing is to have a positive attitude. If you have a positive attitude about yourself, your life, and the people around you, you can be happy and more successful.

The way you get along with your family affects everything else in your life. It helps me to think about treating the people in my family the way I want to be treated. It really pays off to be considerate because a loving family is the best thing a person can have.

Now look back on what you've learned in this course.

❏ Have you learned more about the changes you're experiencing?

❏ Can you identify your own strengths and talents and those of others?

❏ Do you know why it's important to listen and show appreciation to others, including family members?

❏ Can you express your emotions in more positive ways?

❏ Are you more confident about making positive new friends and resisting negative peer pressure?

❏ Have you learned ways to get along better with your family?

❏ Have you practiced developing the skills of thinking critically, solving problems, and making positive, healthy decisions?

❏ Have you learned why and how to resist offers of alcohol, tobacco, marijuana, and other drugs? Have you learned the importance of living healthy and drug-free?

❏ Do you know how to set goals in your life and discover the best within yourself?

If your answer is "Yes" to even one of these questions, you're making progress. You're on your way to becoming the best you can be!

GETTING STARTED

Think about your experiences in *Skills for Adolescence*. Write three words or phrases that describe what you learned, how you feel about the course, or how you feel about yourself after taking the course.

1. _____

_____

2. _____

_____

3. _____

_____

SCRAPBOOK ASSIGNMENT SHEET

NAME: _____ DATE: _____

Answer the questions below to make a scrapbook that shows how the course has helped you. Make the pages from construction paper, cardboard, or plain paper. Add collages, drawings, quotations, poems, or other selections that help explain what you've gained from the course.

PAGE ONE: BEFORE THE COURSE

How would I have described myself?

What kinds of changes did I think I could make in my life?

How did I make decisions and who helped guide me?

What kinds of relationships did I have with my friends and family?

PAGE TWO: DURING THE COURSE

What were the most important things I learned? What skills? Awareness? Attitudes?

What were some high points of the class for me? What skills and positive approaches from the sessions have I tried?

How have my new skills and attitudes improved my relationships with others?

What have I learned about the ways adults can help me reach my goals?

PAGE THREE: IN THE FUTURE

What kind of person do I want to become?

What are my goals?

How will I use the skills I've developed in the course to reach my goals?

Autographs

· ·

Autographs

Autographs

ABOUT THE AUTHORS

 **Gary R. Collins** is a clinical psychologist, psychology teacher, father of two, and internationally known authority on early adolescence. He has written nearly 30 books, including one dealing with teenage stress titled *Give Me a Break*. He is also the author of *The Joy of Caring* and *You Can Profit from Stress*. He consulted with many teenagers in writing his article for this book.

 **Dr. Bill Cosby** has appeared in major television shows and series and is best known for "The Cosby Show." Because of his interest in young people, he earned a doctoral degree in education from the University of Massachusetts. He continues to be involved in youth-oriented programs and is the father of five children.

 **Rick Little** became nationally known as a leader in programs for youth before he finished college. He has inspired thousands of teenagers around the world with a practical, warm, and understanding message. Rick is the founder and chairman of Quest International and has personally helped to implement positive youth development programs for youth in hundreds of schools and communities.

 The late **Peggy Mann** wrote many articles on the health hazards of marijuana, drug abuse among youth, and alcohol, drugs, and driving. One of her articles on the drug problem has been among the *Reader's Digest*'s most frequently requested reprints. She was also well known for writing more than 30 books for young readers. One of her books is titled *Marijuana Alert*.

 **Charlie W. Shedd** is a husband, father, and best-selling author. As a regular columnist for *Teen Magazine*, he has received more than 25,000 letters from teenagers across North America telling about their problems and looking for his help. His books, including *Letters to Karen, Letters to Philip,* and *The Stork Is Dead,* sell by the millions and charm kids and parents alike.

W. Clement Stone is an internationally renowned philanthropist, civic leader, author, publisher, businessman, and Nobel Peace Prize nominee. His philosophy that everyone is capable of success is carried to millions through his speeches, magazine articles, and books such as *Success Through a Positive Mental Attitude* and *A Success System That Never Fails*. His interest in young people led him to offer major support, through the W. Clement and Jessie V. Stone Foundation, to the Lions-Quest *Skills for Adolescence* program.

Barbara Varenhorst is director of the Peer Counseling Program in Palo Alto, California, which pioneered the concept of peer counseling and remains one of the best-known programs of its kind in the country. She is a frequent consultant to school districts and the author of a book for teenagers titled *Real Friends*. Her regular contact with teenagers served as the basis for her article about teenagers and friendship in this book.

Recyclable